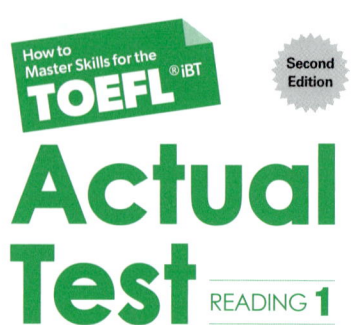

Publisher Kyudo Chung
Editor Inpyo Hong
Authors Michael A. Putlack, Stephen Poirier, Will Link
Proofreader Michael A. Putlack
Designers Minji Kim, Kyuok Chung

First Published in March 2008 By Darakwon, Inc.
Second edition first published in September 2025 by Darakwon, Inc.
Darakwon Bldg., 211, Munbal-ro, Paju-si, Gyeonggi-do 10881
Republic of Korea
Tel: 02-736-2031 (Ext. 250)
Fax: 02-732-2037

Copyright © 2008 Darakwon, 2025 Darakwon

All rights reserved. No part of this publication may be reproduced, stored in a retrieval system, or transmitted in any form or by any means, electronic, mechanical, photocopying or otherwise, without the prior consent of the copyright owner. Refund after purchase is possible only according to the company regulations. Contact the above telephone number for any inquiries. Consumer damages caused by loss, damage, etc. can be compensated according to the consumer dispute resolution standards announced by the Korea Fair Trade Commission. An incorrectly collated book will be exchanged.

ISBN 978-89-277-8108-0 14740
   978-89-277-8105-9 14740 (set)

www.darakwon.co.kr

Photo Credits
Shutterstock.com

Components Main Book / Answer Key / Free MP3 Downloads
7 6 5 4 3 2 1   25 26 27 28 29

Table of **Contents**

Actual Test **01** 009

Actual Test **02** 029

Actual Test **03** 049

Actual Test **04** 069

Actual Test **05** 089

Actual Test **06** 109

Actual Test **07** 129

Actual Test **08** 149

Actual Test **09** 167

Actual Test **10** 187

INTRODUCTION

1 Information on the TOEFL® iBT

A The Format of the TOEFL® iBT

Section	Number of Questions or Tasks	Timing	Score

Reading	**20 Questions**
	• 2 reading passages
	  – with 10 questions per passage
	  – approximately 700 words long each
		35 Minutes	30 Points

Listening	**28 Questions**
	• 2 conversations
	  – 5 questions per conversation
	  – 3 minutes each
	• 3 lectures
	  – 6 questions per lecture
	  – 3-5 minutes each
		36 Minutes	30 Points

Speaking	**4 Tasks**
	• 1 independent speaking task
	  – 1 personal choice/opinion/experience
	  – preparation: 15 sec. / response: 45 sec.
	• 2 integrated speaking tasks: Read-Listen-Speak
	  – 1 campus situation topic
	    reading: 75-100 words (45 sec.)
	    conversation: 150-180 words (60-80 sec.)
	  – 1 academic course topic
	    reading: 75-100 words (50 sec.)
	    lecture: 150-220 words (60-120 sec.)
	  – preparation: 30 sec. / response: 60 sec.
	• 1 integrated speaking task: Listen-Speak
	  – 1 academic course topic
	    lecture: 230-280 words (90-120 sec.)
	  – preparation: 20 sec. / response: 60 sec.
		17 Minutes	30 Points

Writing	**2 Tasks**
	• 1 integrated writing task: Read-Listen-Write
	  – reading: 230-300 words (3 min.)
	  – lecture: 230-300 words (2 min.)
	  – a summary of 150-225 words (20 min.)
	• 1 academic discussion task
	  – a minimum 100-word essay (10 min.)
		30 Minutes	30 Points

B What Is New about the TOEFL® iBT?

- The TOEFL® iBT is delivered through the Internet in secure test centers around the world at the same time.
- It tests all four language skills and is taken in the order of Reading, Listening, Speaking, and Writing.
- The test is about 2 hours long, and all of the four test sections will be completed in one day.
- Note taking is allowed throughout the entire test, including the Reading section. At the end of the test, all notes are collected and destroyed at the test center.
- In the Listening section, one lecture may be spoken with a British or Australian accent.
- There are integrated tasks requiring test takers to combine more than one language skill in the Speaking and Writing sections.
- In the Speaking section, test takers wear headphones and speak into a microphone when they respond. The responses are recorded and transmitted to ETS's Online Scoring Network.
- In the Writing section, test takers must type their responses. Handwriting is not possible.
- Test scores will be reported online. Test takers can see their scores online 4-8 business days after the test and can also receive a copy of their score report by mail.

2 Information on the Reading Section

The Reading section of the TOEFL® iBT measures test takers' ability to understand university-level academic texts. This section has 2 passages, and the length of each passage is about 700 words. Some passages may have underlined words or phrases in blue. Test takers can click on them to see a definition or explanation. Test takers have to answer 10 questions per passage. 35 minutes are given to complete this section, including the time spent reading the passages and answering the questions.

A Types of Reading Passages

- Exposition: Material that provides an explanation of a topic
- Argumentation: Material that presents a point of view about a topic and provides evidence to support it
- Historical narrative: An account of a past event or of a person's life, narrated or written by someone else

B Types of Reading Questions

Type 1 Vocabulary Questions

Vocabulary questions require the test taker to understand specific words or phrases that are used in the passage. These questions ask the test taker to choose another word or phrase that is the most similar in meaning to the highlighted text. The vocabulary words that are highlighted are often important words, so knowing their meanings is often critical for understanding the entire passage. The highlighted words typically have several meanings, so test takers need to be careful to avoid selecting an answer choice simply because it is the word's or phrase's most common meaning.

Type 2 Reference Questions

Reference questions require the test taker to understand the relationship between words and their referents in the passage. These questions most frequently ask the test taker to identify the antecedent of a pronoun. In many cases, the pronouns are words like *he*, *she*, or *they* or *its*, *his*, *hers*, or *theirs*. However, in other cases, relative pronouns like *which* or demonstrative pronouns like *this* or *that* may be asked about instead. This type of question seldom appears on the test anymore.

Type 3 Factual Information Questions

Factual Information questions require the test taker to understand and to be able to recognize facts that are mentioned in the passage. These questions may cover any facts or information that is explicitly covered in the passage. These may appear in the form of details, definitions, explanations, or other kinds of data. The facts which the questions ask about are typically found only in one part of the passage—perhaps in a sentence or two—and do not require a comprehensive understanding of the passage as a whole.

Type 4 Negative Factual Information Questions

Negative Factual Information questions require the test taker to understand and to be able to recognize facts that are mentioned in the passage. These questions may be about any facts or information that is explicitly covered in the passage. However, these questions ask the test taker to identify the incorrect information in the answer choices. Three of the four answer choices will therefore have correct information that can be found in the passage. The answer the test taker must choose will either have incorrect information or information that is not found in the passage.

Type 5 Sentence Simplification Questions

Sentence Simplification questions require the test taker to select a sentence that best restates one that has been highlighted in the passage. These questions ask the test taker to note the main points in the sentence and to make sure that they are mentioned in the rewritten sentence. These sentences use words, phrases, and grammar that are different from the highlighted sentence. They also sometimes do not appear in a passage. When they are asked, there is only one Sentence Simplification question per passage.

Type 6 Inference Questions

Inference questions require the test taker to understand the argument that the passage is attempting to make. These questions ask the test taker to consider the information that is presented and then to come to a logical conclusion about it. The answers to these questions are never explicitly stated in the passage. Instead, the test taker is asked to infer what the author means. These questions often deal with cause and effect or comparisons between two different things, ideas, events, or people.

Type 7 Rhetorical Purpose Questions

Rhetorical Purpose questions require the test taker to understand why the author mentioned or wrote about something in the passage. These questions ask the test taker to consider the reasoning behind the information that is being presented in the passage. For these questions, the function—not the meaning—of the material is the most important aspect to be aware of. The questions often focus on the relationship between the information mentioned or covered either in paragraphs or individual sentences in the passage and the purpose or intention of the information that is given.

Type 8 Insert Text Questions

Insert Text questions require the test taker to determine where in the passage another sentence should be placed. These questions ask the test taker to consider various aspects, including grammar, logic, connecting words, and flow, when deciding where the new sentence best belongs. Recently, there is almost always one Insert Text question per passage. This question always appears just before the last question.

Type 9 Prose Summary Questions

Prose Summary questions require the test taker to understand the main point of the passage and then to select sentences which emphasize the main point. These questions present a sentence which is essentially a thesis statement for the entire passage. The sentence synthesizes the main points of the passage. The test taker must then choose three out of six sentences which most closely describe points mentioned in the introductory sentence. This means that three of the choices are minor points, have incorrect information, or contain information that does not appear in the passage, so they are all therefore incorrect. These are always the last question asked about a Reading passage. Recently, they appear on the test very frequently.

Type 10 Fill in a Table Questions

Fill in a Table questions require the test taker to have a comprehensive understanding of the entire passage. These questions typically break the passage down into two—or sometimes three—main points or themes. The test taker must then read a number of sentences or phrases and determine which of the points or themes the sentences or phrases refer to. These questions often ask the test taker to consider cause and effect, to compare and contrast, or to understand various theories or ideas covered. These are always the last question asked about a Reading passage, but they have become less common recently.

How to Master Skills for the TOEFL® iBT

Actual Test
READING 1

01

TOEFL READING

Reading Section Directions

This section measures your ability to understand academic passages in English. You will have **35 minutes** to read and answer questions about **2 passages**. A clock at the top of the screen will show you how much time is remaining.

Most questions are worth 1 point but the last question for each passage is worth more than 1 point. The directions for the last question indicate how many points you may receive.

Some passages include a word or phrase that is underlined in blue. Click on the word or phrase to see a definition or an explanation.

When you want to move to the next question, click on **Next**. You may skip questions and go back to them later. If you want to return to previous questions, click on **Back**. You can click on **Review** at any time, and the review screen will show you which questions you have answered and which you have not answered. From this review screen, you may go directly to any question you have already seen in the Reading section.

Click on **Continue** to go on.

The Effects of Printing on Society

In 1436, a German goldsmith named Johannes Gutenberg created a device that would revolutionize the world. His invention was the printing press, and while it was not the first device that utilized moveable metal type, it was the first machine in Europe to do so. It dramatically changed Europe first and then other places around the world in various ways for centuries.

Before the printing press, few people in Europe could read. Academics estimate that no more than ten percent of the population was capable of reading at all. The primary reason for this was that there was a dearth of reading material. For centuries, all books were written by hand, which was a laborious process that required a long amount of time and that was expensive because of the cost of **vellum**, which was used to write on, and ink. For instance, a **scribe** might take a year to copy an entire Bible. Handwritten manuscripts were often filled with mistakes as scribes would write down wrong letters or words at times. As a result, there were different versions of the same books due to human error. These books, since they were so difficult to create, were incredibly expensive, so few people could afford to purchase them. For the most part, books were in the possession of nobles, wealthy individuals, monks in monasteries, and other clergymen.

This all changed with Gutenberg's invention. Gutenberg's device allowed for the mass-printing of books, all of which contained the exact same words. This instantly eliminated writing mistakes from books, which allowed people to have more accurate copies. An additional benefit was that the prices of books declined dramatically. For instance, a handwritten Bible in the Middle Ages, the period before Gutenberg made his invention, would have cost a person the equivalent of several thousand dollars in modern times. By the time the Protestant Reformation began in the early sixteenth century, the price of a printed Bible only cost around two or three weeks of wages at that time. Naturally, this led to an increase in the literacy rate since more and more people were able to afford books.

These were not the only benefits of the printing press. In fact, many were quite far reaching. Due to the simplicity of the printing press, people around Europe began making their own devices. Many printing presses were located in large European cities, particularly those with seaports. People not only printed books but also printed manuscripts, pamphlets, and even news reports. In places like Venice, which had one of Europe's greatest maritime fleets, ships' captains would frequently carry books, pamphlets, and news reports to other ports, where they would sell the printed material. This enabled academic works to spread farther and also let people know about various newsworthy events in distant lands. Not only that, but people in the ports where the news reports were sold would reprint them and then take them to towns and cities in other locations. This allowed a much more rapid dissemination of news than had taken place in the past.

When Gutenberg invented the printing press, the Renaissance was going on. This was a time when there was a rebirth of knowledge, primarily from ancient Greece and Rome, going on in Europe. Brilliant men such as Leonardo da Vinci, Nicolaus Copernicus, Galileo Galilei, and Niccolo Machiavelli were making advances in a wide variety of fields. Leonardo, while known primarily as an artist in modern times, was a brilliant engineer and architect. Copernicus and Galileo made discoveries in the field of astronomy while Machiavelli is considered the father of modern political philosophy. Their writings and ideas spread quickly throughout Europe, where they influenced numerous people, thanks to the printing press. William Shakespeare, the English playwright, also lived during the Renaissance, and his plays were printed and shared with people in distant lands.

After the Renaissance came the Reformation, a time when people began breaking with the Catholic Church and formed their own Christian sects, and the Scientific Revolution. These events almost surely would not have happened—or would have happened much more slowly—without the benefit of printing presses to share the ideas people had during those two ages. Clearly, the printing press had a tremendous effect on Europe and its people for centuries after it was invented.

Glossary
vellum: sheep, goat, or cow skin prepared to be written on for a book
scribe: a person who copies manuscripts

The Effects of Printing on Society

¹→ In 1436, a German goldsmith named Johannes Gutenberg created a device that would revolutionize the world. His invention was the printing press, and while it was not the first device that utilized moveable metal type, it was the first machine in Europe to do so. It dramatically changed Europe first and then other places around the world in various ways for centuries.

1. In paragraph 1, all of the following questions are answered EXCEPT:
   A. Where was the printing press the first place to use moveable type?
   B. What method did the printing press use to operate?
   C. When did Johannes Gutenberg complete his important invention?
   D. How did the printing press create various changes in Europe?

²→ Before the printing press, few people in Europe could read. Academics estimate that no more than ten percent of the population was capable of reading at all. The primary reason for this was that there was a dearth of reading material. For centuries, all books were written by hand, which was a laborious process that required a long amount of time and that was expensive because of the cost of **vellum**, which was used to write on, and ink. For instance, a **scribe** might take a year to copy an entire Bible. Handwritten manuscripts were often filled with mistakes as scribes would write down wrong letters or words at times. As a result, there were different versions of the same books due to human error. These books, since they were so difficult to create, were incredibly expensive, so few people could afford to purchase them. For the most part, books were in the possession of nobles, wealthy individuals, monks in monasteries, and other clergymen.

📖 *Glossary*

vellum: sheep, goat, or cow skin prepared to be written on for a book

scribe: a person who copies manuscripts

2. The word "dearth" in the passage is closest in meaning to
   Ⓐ lack
   Ⓑ supply
   Ⓒ presence
   Ⓓ consideration

3. According to paragraph 2, which of the following is true of handwritten manuscripts?
   Ⓐ They were affordable only to members of the nobility.
   Ⓑ They often featured errors due to the scribes that made them.
   Ⓒ They sometimes required up to two years for a person to make.
   Ⓓ They required expensive vellum and cheap ink to create.

³ → This all changed with Gutenberg's invention. Gutenberg's device allowed for the mass-printing of books, all of which contained the exact same words. This instantly eliminated writing mistakes from books, which allowed people to have more accurate copies. An additional benefit was that the prices of books declined dramatically. For instance, a handwritten Bible in the Middle Ages, the period before Gutenberg made his invention, would have cost a person the equivalent of several thousand dollars in modern times. By the time the Protestant Reformation began in the early sixteenth century, the price of a printed Bible only cost around two or three weeks of wages at that time. Naturally, this led to an increase in the literacy rate since more and more people were able to afford books.

4. In paragraph 3, why does the author mention "the Middle Ages"?

Ⓐ To claim that few books were available during that time

Ⓑ To point out how people made books during that period

Ⓒ To argue that few people were literate in medieval times

Ⓓ To make a price comparison with the Protestant Reformation

⁴ ➜ These were not the only benefits of the printing press. In fact, many were quite far reaching. Due to the simplicity of the printing press, people around Europe began making their own devices. Many printing presses were located in large European cities, particularly those with seaports. People not only printed books but also printed manuscripts, pamphlets, and even news reports. In places like Venice, which had one of Europe's greatest maritime fleets, ships' captains would frequently carry books, pamphlets, and news reports to other ports, where they would sell the printed material. This enabled academic works to spread farther and also let people know about various newsworthy events in distant lands. Not only that, but people in the ports where the news reports were sold would reprint them and then take them to towns and cities in other locations. This allowed a much more rapid dissemination of news than had taken place in the past.

5. The word "them" in the passage refers to
   A. various newsworthy events in distant lands
   B. the ports
   C. the news reports
   D. towns and cities

6. In paragraph 4, the author's description of the printing press mentions which of the following?
   A. How much time it took a printing press to make a book
   B. Why many people made their own printing presses
   C. Where the most printing presses were located
   D. Which written material printing presses mostly made

When Gutenberg invented the printing press, the Renaissance was going on. This was a time when there was a rebirth of knowledge, primarily from ancient Greece and Rome, going on in Europe. Brilliant men such as Leonardo da Vinci, Nicolaus Copernicus, Galileo Galilei, and Niccolo Machiavelli were making advances in a wide variety of fields. Leonardo, while known primarily as an artist in modern times, was a brilliant engineer and architect. Copernicus and Galileo made discoveries in the field of astronomy while Machiavelli is considered the father of modern political philosophy. **Their writings and ideas spread quickly throughout Europe, where they influenced numerous people, thanks to the printing press.** William Shakespeare, the English playwright, also lived during the Renaissance, and his plays were printed and shared with people in distant lands.

7. Which of the sentences below best expresses the essential information in the highlighted sentence in the passage? *Incorrect* answer choices change the meaning in important ways or leave out essential information.

   Ⓐ The printing press was one of the most influential inventions in Europe at the time.
   Ⓑ This knowledge went through Europe fast and was influential because of the printing press.
   Ⓒ Because of the printing press, people in Europe got quick access to writings and ideas.
   Ⓓ The printing press enabled people to spread ideas and writings all around Europe.

⁶ ➜ After the Renaissance came the Reformation, a time when people began breaking with the Catholic Church and formed their own Christian sects, and the Scientific Revolution. These events almost surely would not have happened—or would have happened much more slowly—without the benefit of printing presses to share the ideas people had during those two ages. Clearly, the printing press had a tremendous effect on Europe and its people for centuries after it was invented.

8. In paragraph 6, the author implies that the Scientific Revolution

   A. allowed people to enter the modern age of technology
   B. was more important than the Reformation
   C. happened when it did because of the printing press
   D. was a time when the greatest scientific minds lived

These were not the only benefits of the printing press. In fact, many were quite far reaching. Due to the simplicity of the printing press, people around Europe began making their own devices. Many printing presses were located in large European cities, particularly those with seaports. People not only printed books but also printed manuscripts, pamphlets, and even news reports. ■ In places like Venice, which had one of Europe's greatest maritime fleets, ships' captains would frequently carry books, pamphlets, and news reports to other ports, where they would sell the printed material. ■ This enabled academic works to spread farther and also let people know about various newsworthy events in distant lands. ■ Not only that, but people in the ports where the news reports were sold would reprint them and then take them to towns and cities in other locations. ■ This allowed a much more rapid dissemination of news than had taken place in the past.

9. Look at the four squares [■] that indicate where the following sentence could be added to the passage.

The same thing occurred in other port cities, such as Amsterdam and London.

Where would the sentence best fit?

Click on a square [■] to add the sentence to the passage.

10 Directions: An introductory sentence for a brief summary of the passage is provided below. Complete the summary by selecting the THREE answer choices that express the most important ideas of the passage. Some sentences do not belong because they express ideas that are not presented in the passage or are minor ideas in the passage. **This question is worth 2 points.**

Drag your answer choices to the spaces where they belong.
To remove an answer choice, click on it. To review the passage, click on **View Text**.

The printing press influenced Europe in many ways for centuries.

-
-
-

Answer Choices

1. Printing presses in port cities printed material that ships transported.
2. Johannes Gutenberg used moveable type to make his printing press.
3. The ideas of the Renaissance spread at a very rapid rate.
4. The literacy rate increased as books became cheaper and more plentiful.
5. William Shakespeare's works were spread thanks to the printing press.
6. The Reformation and the Scientific Revolution were able to take place.

The Chimpanzee

Chimpanzees in Kibale National Park, Uganda

The groundbreaking work of primatologists Louis Leakey and Jane Goodall has shown that the chimpanzee is not just another monkey. On the contrary, their astonishing research reveals that these primates exhibit numerous highly developed physical as well as mental characteristics that were previously thought only to be innate in humans. Goodall herself was one of the first people to recognize or realize the chimpanzee's ability to use tools, which, at the time, caused near **pandemonium** in the scientific world because experts believed only humans were able to do this. It is also now known due to recent hi-tech research that the chimpanzee's DNA makeup mirrors the genetic mapping of *Homo sapiens* to within a few chromosomes or so of being identical. Regardless of these similarities, the chimpanzee's entire existence is being seriously threatened by its more complex peer: man.

Critical and fundamental to any living organisms on the planet is their habitats, and chimpanzees are no exception. When it comes to the chimpanzee, trees are key, and without them, they are, for the most part, headed for extinction. Chimpanzees are indigenous to Africa, where the tree canopy provides them with shelter, food, and protection. For example, chimpanzees are omnivorous, which means that they rely on meat, plant life, and fruit for subsistence. They also take refuge in trees when they feel threatened by predators or violent storms and flooding. Without trees, chimpanzees will become vulnerable to nature's forces and will lack the necessary food sources to keep them viable. What is so worrisome is that acre upon acre of the chimpanzee's habitat is being hacked to the ground every single day.

The deforestation of the jungle in Africa for profit and space is the single biggest threat to the chimpanzee's immediate and future livelihood. Because of skyrocketing populations and the paucity of housing in many regions of Africa, developers are cutting back the jungle to make room for new communities while simultaneously uprooting and displacing the chimpanzee. It seems that they have no regard at all for their primate neighbors, which eventually become isolated from one another in separate tiny patchworks of trees. When groups of chimpanzees become fragmented and isolated from one another, their own genetic makeup is placed in jeopardy because they are not able to share genetic information. This isolation can have a very profound effect on future generations of chimpanzees if they even make it that far. Some experts are even predicting that, within twenty years, over eighty percent of the chimpanzee's habitat could be lost to development and brutal clear-cutting tactics.

The domino effect continues from the threat of deforestation to that of disease. As human populations begin to tread on the chimpanzee's habitat, man and primate come into closer contact with each other, exposing the chimpanzee to all kinds of human diseases ranging from the common cold to pneumonia to AIDS. The problem is that chimpanzees have no natural immunity to human-borne diseases, so what may be just a sore throat and a cough to a human could prove fatal to a chimpanzee. As human populations in Africa explode and encroach on chimpanzee societies, they begin to become infected with diseases, suffer, and die. If something is not done to protect the chimpanzee's habitat and to separate chimpanzees from human populations, their fate is all but sealed.

One final factor which threatens the existence of the chimpanzee is the thriving live animal trade in Africa as well as the demand for them throughout the world. To many people, chimpanzees are simply cute, furry, exotic animals—the perfect addition to a home. Infant chimpanzees are taken from their mothers and sold on the black market, which further decreases their numbers in the wild. The truth is that while chimpanzees should never be stripped from the jungle, they are additionally wild animals and do not make obedient, domesticated pets. The live animal trade only puts money in the pockets of senseless individuals interested in nothing more than their own gains. Without continual pressure of governmental and environmental groups and the implementation of stricter guidelines, which regulate and thwart the destruction of the chimpanzee's habitat, they may soon be another animal lost for eternity to human greed.

Glossary
pandemonium: a situation in which there is a lot of noise and confusion

The Chimpanzee

1 → The groundbreaking work of primatologists Louis Leakey and Jane Goodall has shown that the chimpanzee is not just another monkey. On the contrary, their astonishing research reveals that these primates exhibit numerous highly developed physical as well as mental characteristics that were previously thought only to be **innate** in humans. Goodall herself was one of the first people to recognize or realize the chimpanzee's ability to use tools, which, at the time, caused near **pandemonium** in the scientific world because experts believed only humans were able to do this. It is also now known due to recent hi-tech research that the chimpanzee's DNA makeup mirrors the genetic mapping of *Homo sapiens* to within a few chromosomes or so of being identical. Regardless of these similarities, the chimpanzee's entire existence is being seriously threatened by its more complex peer: man.

Glossary

pandemonium: a situation in which there is a lot of noise and confusion

11. The word "innate" in the passage is closest in meaning to
    Ⓐ extrinsic
    Ⓑ relevant
    Ⓒ found
    Ⓓ inborn

12. According to paragraph 1, chimpanzees are unique because
    Ⓐ primatologist Jane Goodall was able to dedicate her life to their study
    Ⓑ they display many abilities reminiscent of certain traits of human beings
    Ⓒ their genetic makeup is a perfect match to that of *Homo sapiens*
    Ⓓ they have been able to avoid extinction, unlike many of their cousin primates

2 → Critical and fundamental to any living organisms on the planet is their habitats, and chimpanzees are no exception. When it comes to the chimpanzee, trees are key, and without them, they are, for the most part, headed for extinction. Chimpanzees are indigenous to Africa, where the tree canopy provides them with shelter, food, and protection. For example, chimpanzees are omnivorous, which means that they rely on meat, vegetation, and fruit for subsistence. They also take refuge in trees when they feel threatened by predators or violent storms and flooding. Without trees, chimpanzees will become vulnerable to nature's forces and will lack the necessary food sources to keep them viable. What is so worrisome is that acre upon acre of the chimpanzee's habitat is being hacked to the ground every single day.

13. Which of the following can be inferred from paragraph 2 about habitats?
    - A. Chimpanzees are very adaptable to different habitats depending on their needs.
    - B. The tree canopy in the jungle is the basis of the chimpanzee's habitat.
    - C. They do not change but force animal species to adapt to them.
    - D. They will disappear once the animals living in them become extinct.

14. The author discusses "trees" in paragraph 2 in order to
    - A. emphasize the dire need to reform timber-clearing tactics threatening the chimpanzee
    - B. show how violent flooding will increase with the further reduction of trees in the wild
    - C. tell how many trees are being cut down in the chimpanzee's habitat in Africa
    - D. point out that because of clear-cutting tactics, chimpanzees will become more isolated

The deforestation of the jungle in Africa for profit and space is the single biggest threat to the chimpanzee's immediate and future livelihood. Because of skyrocketing populations and the paucity of housing in many regions of Africa, developers are cutting back the jungle to make room for new communities while simultaneously uprooting and displacing the chimpanzee. It seems that they have no regard at all for their primate neighbors, which eventually become isolated from one another in separate tiny patchworks of trees. When groups of chimpanzees become fragmented and isolated from one another, their own genetic makeup is placed in jeopardy because they are not able to share genetic information. This isolation can have a very profound effect on future generations of chimpanzees if they even make it that far. Some experts are even predicting that, within twenty years, over eighty percent of the chimpanzee's habitat could be lost to development and brutal clear-cutting tactics.

15 Which of the sentences below best expresses the essential information in the highlighted sentence in the passage? *Incorrect* answer choices change the meaning in important ways or leave out essential information.

Ⓐ The isolation of chimpanzees reduces diversity in their genetic pool, which can be detrimental.

Ⓑ As chimpanzees become fragmented from one another, they begin to lose their genetic identity.

Ⓒ Genetic information is passed on to isolated groups of chimpanzees from roaming individuals.

Ⓓ Jeopardizing genetics will result in chimpanzees becoming more isolated and fragmented.

4 ⇒ The domino effect continues from the threat of deforestation to that of disease. As human populations begin to tread on the chimpanzee's habitat, man and primate come into closer contact with each other, exposing the chimpanzee to all kinds of human diseases ranging from the common cold to pneumonia to AIDS. The problem is that chimpanzees have no natural immunity to human-borne diseases, so what may be just a sore throat and a cough to a human could prove fatal to a chimpanzee. As human populations in Africa explode and encroach on chimpanzee societies, they begin to become infected with diseases, suffer, and die. If something is not done to protect the chimpanzee's habitat and to separate chimpanzees from human populations, their fate is all but sealed.

16 According to paragraph 4, disease is affecting chimpanzees because

(A) their immune systems are suffering from unhealthy diets

(B) their natural immunities against diseases are being compromised

(C) their habitats are getting occupied by various groups of people

(D) the AIDS virus is fatal to them as much as it is for human beings

17 The phrase "encroach on" in the passage is closest in meaning to

(A) invade

(B) dominate

(C) tempt

(D) surround

5 → One final factor which threatens the existence of the chimpanzee is the thriving live animal trade in Africa as well as the demand for them throughout the world. To many people, chimpanzees are simply cute, furry, exotic animals—the perfect addition to a home. Infant chimpanzees are taken from their mothers and sold on the black market, which further decreases their numbers in the wild. ■[1] The truth is that while chimpanzees should never be stripped from the jungle, they are additionally wild animals and do not make obedient, domesticated pets. ■[2] The live animal trade only puts money in the pockets of senseless individuals interested in nothing more than their own gains. ■[3] Without continual pressure of governmental and environmental groups and the implementation of stricter guidelines, which regulate and thwart the destruction of the chimpanzee's habitat, they may soon be another animal lost for eternity to human greed. ■[4]

18 According to paragraph 5, the live animal trade of the chimpanzee occurs because

- Ⓐ the temperaments of baby chimpanzees make them become excellent pets
- Ⓑ buying and selling chimpanzees is more lucrative than the trade of other animals
- Ⓒ there is a high demand for chimpanzees by certain ignorant and careless people
- Ⓓ there are large populations of baby chimpanzees taken from their mothers

19 Look at the four squares [■] that indicate where the following sentence could be added to the passage.

Furthermore, once these young chimpanzees get older and the novelty of owning them wears off, they are abandoned by their owners.

Where would the sentence best fit?

Click on a square [■] to add the sentence to the passage.

20 Directions: An introductory sentence for a brief summary of the passage is provided below. Complete the summary by selecting the THREE answer choices that express the most important ideas of the passage. Some sentences do not belong because they express ideas that are not presented in the passage or are minor ideas in the passage. **This question is worth 2 points.**

Drag your answer choices to the spaces where they belong.
To remove an answer choice, click on it. To review the passage, click on **View Text**.

The livelihood of the chimpanzee is being placed in jeopardy for a number of important reasons.

-
-
-

Answer Choices

1. Trees are chimpanzees' main source of food as well as a form of protection for them.
2. Chimpanzees are cute and furry and are considered by many to be exotic animals.
3. The chimpanzee is native to many different areas on the African continent.
4. Because they are favored as pets, the population of chimpanzees is being compromised.
5. Chimpanzees have not been observed by anyone using tools for any purposes.
6. The development of industry is destroying chimpanzees' habitats at an alarming rate.

How to Master Skills for the TOEFL® iBT

Actual Test
READING 1

02

TOEFL READING

Reading Section Directions

This section measures your ability to understand academic passages in English. You will have **35 minutes** to read and answer questions about **2 passages**. A clock at the top of the screen will show you how much time is remaining.

Most questions are worth 1 point but the last question for each passage is worth more than 1 point. The directions for the last question indicate how many points you may receive.

Some passages include a word or phrase that is **underlined** in blue. Click on the word or phrase to see a definition or an explanation.

When you want to move to the next question, click on **Next**. You may skip questions and go back to them later. If you want to return to previous questions, click on **Back**. You can click on **Review** at any time, and the review screen will show you which questions you have answered and which you have not answered. From this review screen, you may go directly to any question you have already seen in the Reading section.

Click on **Continue** to go on.

Space Settlements

The United States government is taking a serious look at the moon and Mars as potential places for future human settlement for various reasons. First, they could be future sources of natural resources desperately needed on Earth. Second, the moon could serve as a training ground or a stepping stone for later journeys to Mars. Therefore, the moon is already on NASA's **docket** for further exploration within the next couple of decades, which, at least to some experts, is completely unnecessary mainly due to the needless risks involved. With Mars looming as the eventual long-term goal, serious questions exist as to whether the dangers and difficulties of a lunar settlement are too extreme and unnecessary. The moon's relatively harsh environment and the greater potential of natural resources on Mars are major reasons that make lunar settlements too great a liability and why the moon should be bypassed.

One major reason a lunar settlement is too hazardous is the contrast between the environments of the moon and the Red Planet. Numerous scientists believe the moon is too difficult for human settlement as compared to Mars. The fact that the moon has no atmosphere poses the greatest threat to humans. Atmosphere is crucial because it protects humans and all life from continuous bombardment of cosmic radiation caused by sources such as the sun. This radiation is especially dangerous to humans because it increases the risk of cancer and can negatively alter and mutate DNA. On the other hand, while Mars's atmosphere is significantly thinner than Earth's, at least it has one and would create a slight protective barrier for humans.

Another important characteristic necessary for sustainable human settlement is water, of which the moon is believed to have none. If lunar settlements are to be successful, water will be a key component and must be brought with the colonists and continually supplied by further expeditions from Earth, which means they will have a limited capacity of it. Conversely, Mars contains vast quantities of water ice, dry ice, and also snow. There is also ample evidence that water once existed on Mars's surface and might return in the future if the planet warms. With increased technological advances in conversion capabilities, the potential for settlers to remain on Mars indefinitely by being increasingly self-sufficient makes Mars a much more attractive goal as a space colony than the moon.

Future colonists will not only benefit from potential water sources on Mars; the planet is also rich in other basic elements vital to sustaining life. These include nitrogen, oxygen, and hydrogen. Mars also contains many minerals that contain iron, silicon, and magnesium, which can be used productively. For example, silicon can be utilized to make solar cells to store energy and to create electricity. Hydrogen can be extracted from water sources and employed as fuel. Moreover, it can be combined with nitrogen to form fertilizing materials necessary to a sustainable colony. Due to these factors, Mars would be a more successful candidate for exploration and settlement because it contains the basic resources necessary for humans to survive more independently of aid from Earth than they would on the moon.

Clearly, any future settlements on Mars or the moon will be monumental efforts for the space agencies and astronauts involved. The expenses incurred will be extreme and are a further reason why plans and implementation should focus on the project, which has the greater potential of long-term success. While the moon may serve as a temporary training ground for Mars, it could end up becoming a major diversion from Mars and place humans in too great a risk with too little benefit. Because the environment of Mars is more similar to that of Earth and it contains important resources necessary to sustain life, it should be the one and only option for any kind of long-term human settlement. Furthermore, the moon has been eclipsed by mankind, so it is only natural that Mars be the next step for space exploration. Finally, the habitation of Mars would not only be a milestone in space but also an excellent opportunity for mankind to redeem itself from past exploits on Earth and to preserve and make the best use of the natural resources Mars has to offer.

Glossary
docket: a list of things to be done; an agenda

Space Settlements

¹→ The United States government is taking a serious look at the moon and Mars as potential places for future human settlement for various reasons. First, they could be future sources of natural resources desperately needed on Earth. Second, the moon could serve as a training ground or a stepping stone for later journeys to Mars. Therefore, the moon is already on NASA's **docket** for further exploration within the next couple of decades, which, at least to some experts, is completely unnecessary mainly due to the needless risks involved. With Mars **looming** as the eventual long-term goal, serious questions exist as to whether the dangers and difficulties of a lunar settlement are too extreme and unnecessary. The moon's relatively harsh environment and the greater potential of natural resources on Mars are major reasons that make lunar settlements too great a liability and why the moon should be bypassed.

Glossary
docket: a list of things to be done; an agenda

1. The word "looming" in the passage is closest in meaning to
   - Ⓐ expanding
   - Ⓑ competing
   - Ⓒ waiting
   - Ⓓ emerging

2. According to paragraph 1, which of the following is true of space settlements?
   - Ⓐ They should have already been instigated by NASA many years ago.
   - Ⓑ They must first incorporate the moon as a practice arena for Mars exploration.
   - Ⓒ They could prove to be a last resort for gaining life-sustaining supplies.
   - Ⓓ Their danger cannot be justified due to the risk to human life and the high cost.

2 → One major reason a lunar settlement is too hazardous is the contrast between the environments of the moon and the Red Planet. Numerous scientists believe the moon is too difficult for human settlement as compared to Mars. The fact that the moon has no atmosphere poses the greatest threat to humans. Atmosphere is crucial because it protects humans and all life from continuous bombardment of cosmic radiation caused by sources such as the sun. This radiation is especially dangerous to humans because it increases the risk of cancer and can negatively alter and mutate DNA. On the other hand, while Mars's atmosphere is significantly thinner than Earth's, at least it has one and would create a slight protective barrier for humans.

3. The author discusses "environments" in paragraph 2 in order to

   A) justify why the moon is a more practical place than Mars for human settlement
   B) express the notion that Mars poses fewer life-threatening hazards than the moon
   C) propose that cosmic radiation would have little effect on the lunar colonists
   D) indicate that lunar settlements are futile because the moon has no atmosphere

4. According to paragraph 2, the atmosphere on Mars would

   A) change the genetic makeup of humans and cause their DNA to mutate
   B) protect humans completely from harmful cosmic radiation coming from space
   C) cause humans to be more openly exposed to potentially fatal illnesses
   D) give human colonists a safety shield against dangerous cosmic effects

Another important characteristic necessary for sustainable human settlement is water, of which the moon is believed to have none. If lunar settlements are to be successful, water will be a key component and must be brought with the colonists and continually supplied by further expeditions from Earth, which means they will have a limited capacity of it. Conversely, Mars contains vast quantities of water ice, dry ice, and also snow. There is also ample evidence that water once existed on Mars's surface and might return in the future if the planet warms. With increased technological advances in conversion capabilities, the potential for settlers to remain on Mars indefinitely by being increasingly self-sufficient makes Mars a much more attractive goal as a space colony than the moon.

5. Which of the sentences below best expresses the essential information in the highlighted sentence in the passage? *Incorrect* answer choices change the meaning in important ways or leave out essential information.

Ⓐ The moon is easier to adapt to because of advances in technology and self-sufficiency.

Ⓑ Having settlers staying on Mars is more appealing because of its potential as a colony.

Ⓒ Mars may be a better long-term option than the moon because of the most recent technology.

Ⓓ Conversion capabilities will enable settlers to make traveling to the moon a more viable goal.

⁴ ➔ Future colonists will not only benefit from potential water sources on Mars; the planet is also rich in other basic elements vital to sustaining life. These include nitrogen, oxygen, and hydrogen. Mars also contains many minerals that contain iron, silicon, and magnesium, which can be used productively. For example, silicon can be utilized to make solar cells to store energy and to create electricity. Hydrogen can be extracted from water sources and employed as fuel. Moreover, it can be combined with nitrogen to form fertilizing materials necessary to a sustainable colony. Due to these factors, Mars would be a more successful candidate for exploration and settlement because it contains the basic resources necessary for humans to survive more independently of aid from Earth than they would on the moon.

6. In paragraph 4, what can be inferred about water sources on Mars?
   Ⓐ They exist in liquid form below the surface and ice at the immediate surface.
   Ⓑ They are not present at the moment though they probably once were.
   Ⓒ They can be easily converted into liquid forms necessary for life.
   Ⓓ They are not known to be present in a fluid state above or below the surface.

7. The word "fertilizing" in the passage is closest in meaning to
   Ⓐ nourishing
   Ⓑ exhausting
   Ⓒ suffocating
   Ⓓ saturating

5 → Clearly, any future settlements on Mars or the moon will be monumental efforts for the space agencies and astronauts involved. The expenses incurred will be extreme and are a further reason why plans and implementation should focus on the project, which has the greater potential of long-term success. While the moon may serve as a temporary training ground for Mars, it could end up becoming a major diversion from Mars and place humans in too great a risk with too little benefit. Because the environment of Mars is more similar to that of Earth and it contains important resources necessary to sustain life, it should be the one and only option for any kind of long-term human settlement. Furthermore, the moon has been eclipsed by mankind, so it is only natural that Mars be the next step for space exploration. Finally, the habitation of Mars would not only be a milestone in space but also an excellent opportunity for mankind to redeem itself from past exploits on Earth and to preserve and make the best use of the natural resources Mars has to offer.

8. According to paragraph 5, what is a factor against moon settlements?

   Ⓐ Astronauts must be able to multitask and will be far away from life-saving aid.
   Ⓑ Since the moon contains no trace of water, it must be brought from Earth.
   Ⓒ Funding for them will take away from the resources appropriated to Mars missions.
   Ⓓ The lack of weather and gravity will have a negative effect on future colonists.

Another important characteristic necessary for sustainable human settlement is water, of which the moon is believed to have none. ■ If lunar settlements are to be successful, water will be a key component and must be brought with the colonists and continually supplied by further expeditions from Earth, which means they will have a limited capacity of it. ■ Conversely, Mars contains vast quantities of water ice, dry ice, and also snow. ■ There is also ample evidence that water once existed on Mars's surface and might return in the future if the planet warms. ■ With increased technological advances in conversion capabilities, the potential for settlers to remain on Mars indefinitely by being increasingly self-sufficient makes Mars a much more attractive goal as a space colony than the moon.

9. Look at the four squares [■] that indicate where the following sentence could be added to the passage.

If supplies are delayed for one reason or another, the entire project and the livelihoods of the colonists could be in serious jeopardy.

Where would the sentence best fit?

Click on a square [■] to add the sentence to the passage.

Directions: An introductory sentence for a brief summary of the passage is provided below. Complete the summary by selecting the THREE answer choices that express the most important ideas of the passage. Some sentences do not belong because they express ideas that are not presented in the passage or are minor ideas in the passage. **This question is worth 2 points.**

Drag your answer choices to the spaces where they belong.
To remove an answer choice, click on it. To review the passage, click on **View Text**.

Settlements on Mars would be challenging like those on Earth's moon, yet they would be able to sustain life much better.

-
-
-

Answer Choices

1. The moon would provide an excellent training ground for future expeditions to Mars.
2. The environment of Mars would be more receptive to humans than that of the moon.
3. Rich in nitrogen and hydrogen, the moon can sustain life more easily than Mars.
4. Potential sources of water on Mars make it a better long-term option.
5. Long-term exposure to radiation on an atmosphere-less Mars could prove fatal.
6. Minerals found on Mars can help colonists create independent energy sources.

The Toraja

A traditional Toraja cemetery on a hillside

  Funeral rites have always played important roles in human history. They typically symbolize a kind of closure of an individual's life on the Earth and provide family and friends the opportunity to pay their respects and to say goodbye. There are many different kinds of funeral ceremonies around the world. The funeral tradition of the Toraja people on the island of Sulawesi in Indonesia is like no other as it blends the Toraja's ancient animist beliefs with the western influences of Christianity. To the Toraja, death is a new beginning as the deceased pass from the restrictions of this life into the afterlife, where they will oversee and conduct the lives of the people they have left behind. But before this can occur, an elaborate funeral celebration must take place. This celebration, as well as their treatment of the dead, separates the traditions of the Toraja from most modern cultures.

  The first noticeable difference between Torajan funerals and Western ones is how they prepare for them. The Toraja often begin preparing for their family members' funerals well before they actually die. Sometimes they even start preparations before the member falls ill. In most Western cultures, this is unheard of since most funeral preparations are made immediately following death. This is not so for the Toraja. The reason is mainly due to cost since a family may incur heavy expenses when they attempt to send their family member into the afterlife in the most celebrative, festive, and prepared manner possible.

  Interestingly, the Toraja do not relate to death in its physical form. They believe that when a family member dies, only his physical form has ceased to function. They consider the essence of the individual eternal and believe it will continue to exist in this world until a proper funeral ceremony has been performed to send that person off to the next stage of existence. Because of this, the deceased are simply wrapped up and kept in the house, called a *tongkonan*, until the time of celebration. During this in-between period, the deceased is treated as if he were still alive. The rest of the family holds conversations with him and even feeds him. Death then is not an end but the beginning of the passage into the afterlife. Dying also does not take an individual away for the Toraja. They believe they are in complete control of that aspect, and only through celebrations and feasts are they able to break the limbo of their family member.

An elaborate funeral celebration is also important to impress the gods with the individual's worldly importance and wealth. Water buffalo, which represent both financial success and status in society, are crucial to Torajan culture. During a funeral celebration, a number of water buffalo are sacrificed in accordance with the person's level in the Torajan hierarchy. But water buffaloes are not cheap, especially for the Toraja, who are mainly subsistence farmers. Therefore, a family must work months—or sometimes years—to save enough money to purchase a satisfactory number of water buffaloes and other animals, such as pigs, for the funeral ceremony. Once all is in order, a date for the celebration is set so that friends and members of the community bearing gifts can visit. Large quantities of food and **libations** are consumed during festivities involving sports, dancing, and storytelling, which usually continue for a week.

With the cycle in full force, the climax occurs at the end of the feast, when the body is placed in a coffin and carried to its final resting place, which is not in the ground but high up above it. Traditional Toraja cemeteries are located in the side of a cliff, where hollowed-out sections are made for families and individuals. The body is placed in a horizontal vault and enclosed with stone or wood. This, however, does not mean that the deceased is sealed off from his homeland. A wooden **effigy** of the individual, called a *tau tau*, is placed at the entrance of the tomb to guard it and to protect living family members. *Tau tau* are additionally thought to bestow prosperity on the Toraja in general as well as connect them with deceased family members and gods beyond.

Glossary
libation: an alcoholic drink
effigy: a crude figure or statue of a person

The Toraja

1 → Funeral rites have always played important roles in human history. They typically symbolize a kind of closure of an individual's life on the Earth and provide family and friends the opportunity to pay their respects and to say goodbye. There are many different kinds of funeral ceremonies around the world. The funeral tradition of the Toraja people on the island of Sulawesi in Indonesia is like no other as it blends the Toraja's ancient animist beliefs with the western influences of Christianity. To the Toraja, death is a new beginning as the deceased pass from the restrictions of this life into the afterlife, where they will oversee and conduct the lives of the people they have left behind. But before this can occur, an elaborate funeral celebration must take place. This celebration, as well as their treatment of the dead, separates the traditions of the Toraja from most modern cultures.

11 Why does the author mention "Christianity" in paragraph 1?

- (A) To indicate a shift in belief from ancient and modern Toraja
- (B) To contrast both Christian and animist funeral traditions
- (C) To reveal how the Toraja have adapted it to their own culture
- (D) To question if it is appropriate for Western influence to affect the Toraja

12 According to paragraph 1, most humans have funeral ceremonies because they

- (A) create a sense of finality for the families and friends involved in the event
- (B) give loved ones an opportunity to spend more time with distant family members
- (C) follow a strict code which will successfully send the deceased into the afterlife
- (D) are necessary in cultures that have followed animist beliefs for centuries

² → The first noticeable difference between Torajan funerals and Western ones is how they prepare for them. The Toraja often begin preparing for their family members' funerals well before they actually die. Sometimes they even start preparations before the member falls ill. In most Western cultures, this is unheard of since most funeral preparations are made immediately following death. This is not so for the Toraja. The reason is mainly due to cost since a family may incur heavy expenses when they attempt to send their family member into the afterlife in the most celebrative, festive, and prepared manner possible.

13 The word "incur" in the passage is closest in meaning to
- Ⓐ spare
- Ⓑ extract
- Ⓒ sustain
- Ⓓ withstand

14 According to paragraph 2, Torajan funerals are unique because
- Ⓐ the Toraja prepare for the funeral only months after someone dies
- Ⓑ preparations begin while the individual it is for is still alive and well
- Ⓒ the Toraja organize the funeral immediately after an individual passes away
- Ⓓ everyone in the society contributes to the financing of the funeral

Interestingly, the Toraja do not relate to death in its physical form. They believe that when a family member dies, only his physical form has ceased to function. They consider the essence of the individual eternal and believe it will continue to exist in this world until a proper funeral ceremony has been performed to send that person off to the next stage of existence. Because of this, the deceased are simply wrapped up and kept in the house, called a *tongkonan*, until the time of celebration. During this in-between period, the deceased is treated as if he were still alive. The rest of the family holds conversations with him and even feeds him. Death then is not an end but the beginning of the passage into the afterlife. Dying also does not take an individual away for the Toraja. They believe they are in complete control of that aspect, and only through celebrations and feasts are they able to break the limbo of their family member.

15 Which of the sentences below best expresses the essential information in the highlighted sentence in the passage? *Incorrect* answer choices change the meaning in important ways or leave out essential information.

- Ⓐ The funeral is the vehicle that allows the deceased individual to enter the next stage of his life.
- Ⓑ The deceased individual will linger in this world until he is prepared to enter the next one.
- Ⓒ After a proper ceremony is performed, the individual becomes immortal and enters the afterlife.
- Ⓓ The afterlife is attained only after an individual has given up his worldly ties with a funeral.

⁴ ➜ An elaborate funeral celebration is also important to impress the gods with the individual's worldly importance and wealth. Water buffalo, which represent both financial success and status in society, are crucial to Torajan culture. During a funeral celebration, a number of water buffalo are sacrificed in accordance with the person's level in the Torajan hierarchy. But water buffaloes are not cheap, especially for the Toraja, who are mainly subsistence farmers. Therefore, a family must work months—or sometimes years—to save enough money to purchase a satisfactory number of water buffaloes and other animals, such as pigs, for the funeral ceremony. Once all is in order, a date for the celebration is set so that friends and members of the community bearing gifts can visit. Large quantities of food and **libations** are consumed during festivities involving sports, dancing, and storytelling, which usually continue for a week.

16 Which of the following can be inferred from paragraph 4 about funeral celebrations?

Ⓐ They are a welcome time for the families that are involved in them.

Ⓑ Families are under great pressure to raise money for them.

Ⓒ The Toraja believe their gods are only pleased by sacrificing buffaloes.

Ⓓ Many of the Toraja are boycotting funerals because of the slaughter.

📖 ***Glossary***
libation: an alcoholic drink

5 → With the cycle in full force, the climax occurs at the end of the feast, when the body is placed in a coffin and carried to its final resting place, which is not in the ground but high up above it. Traditional Toraja cemeteries are located in the side of a cliff, where hollowed-out sections are made for families and individuals. The body is placed in a horizontal vault and enclosed with stone or wood. This, however, does not mean that the deceased is sealed off from his homeland. A wooden **effigy** of the individual, called a *tau tau*, is placed at the entrance of the tomb to guard it and to protect living family members. *Tau tau* are additionally thought to bestow prosperity on the Toraja in general as well as connect them with deceased family members and gods beyond.

17. According to paragraph 5, which of the following is NOT true of the author's description of Toraja cemeteries?

    Ⓐ *Tau tau* are the guardians of the tombs.
    Ⓑ They are located in the sides of hills or mountains.
    Ⓒ Deceased bodies are entombed at the ends of feasts.
    Ⓓ The deceased are always buried in individual tombs.

18. According to paragraph 5, the Toraja place *tau tau* at the entrance of the tomb to

    Ⓐ speak to family members when they visit the deceased
    Ⓑ bring fortune to the entire society of the Toraja
    Ⓒ keep other deceased family members company
    Ⓓ remind visitors what the deceased looked like in their primes

📖 ***Glossary***
effigy: a crude figure or statue of a person

The first noticeable difference between Torajan funerals and Western ones is how they prepare for them. The Toraja often begin preparing for their family members' funerals well before they actually die. ■ Sometimes they even start preparations before the member falls ill. ■ In most Western cultures, this is unheard of since most funeral preparations are made immediately following death. ■ This is not so for the Toraja. ■ The reason is mainly due to cost since a family may incur heavy expenses when they attempt to send their family member into the afterlife in the most celebrative, festive, and prepared manner possible.

19. Look at the four squares [■] that indicate where the following sentence could be added to the passage.

Furthermore, it would probably be considered a bad omen by most people were a person to engage in this kind of behavior.

Where would the sentence best fit?

Click on a square [■] to add the sentence to the passage.

20 Directions: An introductory sentence for a brief summary of the passage is provided below. Complete the summary by selecting the THREE answer choices that express the most important ideas of the passage. Some sentences do not belong because they express ideas that are not presented in the passage or are minor ideas in the passage. **This question is worth 2 points.**

Drag your answer choices to the spaces where they belong.
To remove an answer choice, click on it. To review the passage, click on **View Text**.

The lengthy funeral ceremony of the Toraja releases the deceased to the next level of their existence.

-
-
-

Answer Choices

1. The number of cows slaughtered at the celebration depends on the person's wealth.
2. The Toraja view death as a new beginning rather than an end for the individual.
3. Funeral preparations are made days in advance of a family member's impending death.
4. The funeral celebration of the Toraja represents the person's success in life.
5. Friends and family members bring gifts to the funeral celebration as a condolence.
6. Toraja funerals are festive times of eating and games and can last as long as a week.

Actual Test
READING 1

03

TOEFL READING

Reading Section Directions

This section measures your ability to understand academic passages in English. You will have **35 minutes** to read and answer questions about **2 passages**. A clock at the top of the screen will show you how much time is remaining.

Most questions are worth 1 point but the last question for each passage is worth more than 1 point. The directions for the last question indicate how many points you may receive.

Some passages include a word or phrase that is **underlined** in blue. Click on the word or phrase to see a definition or an explanation.

When you want to move to the next question, click on **Next**. You may skip questions and go back to them later. If you want to return to previous questions, click on **Back**. You can click on **Review** at any time, and the review screen will show you which questions you have answered and which you have not answered. From this review screen, you may go directly to any question you have already seen in the Reading section.

Click on **Continue** to go on.

Mangrove Forests

A mangrove forest in Malayisa

 Few trees are able to survive in **brackish** water, yet the approximately eighty species of mangrove trees thrive in this kind of environment. Mangroves are typically found growing along coastlines in tropical and subtropical conditions. These trees grow closely together, and their roots, many of which grow aboveground, combine to form thick tangles referred to as mangrove forests. Mangrove forests are extremely vital to their local environments for a number of reasons.

 Due to the diversity of mangrove species, some may only grow around 1.5 meters in height, making them shrubs, whereas others may rise forty meters or more high. Despite these differences in size, all mangroves share the ability to live in salty water and low oxygen conditions. One adaptation that permits mangroves to thrive is that they have defenses protecting them from salt in water. Some, called non-secreters, create barriers that prevent salt from being absorbed through the process of **osmosis**, which is how they take in water. Other mangroves, known as secreters, take in salt along with the water they absorb but then undergo a process to remove the salt through pores or salt glands located in their leaves. This capability permits some mangroves to grow in water containing two times the salt content of the ocean.

 A second adaptation that benefits mangroves is root aeration, which enables them to survive in soil without oxygen. While mangroves undergo photosynthesis to create energy for themselves, they still require oxygen for their cells. Most trees simply absorb oxygen from gases found in the soil, but because mangrove roots are flooded with water, they have undergone adaptations to enable them to access oxygen. Some mangroves have aboveground roots that rise above the water level and therefore enable the plant to obtain oxygen from the air. Some of these roots, which can be quite high, keep the trunks of mangroves entirely above water while also providing stability for the trees.

Most mangroves grow between twenty-five degrees latitude north and twenty-five degrees latitude south, which is the area close to the equator. There are vast expanses of mangrove forests on the coasts of Central and South America, Africa, the Middle East, India, Southeast Asia, and Australia. These are all places which see frequent tropical storms such as hurricanes, typhoons, and cyclones. When powerful tropical storms—and also tsunamis caused by undersea earthquakes—send storm surges toward shore, mangrove forests are effective at mitigating their effects. The facts that the trees grow closely together and have complex aboveground root structures help reduce the sizes of waves approaching the shore. While strong winds may knock some trees over and break off branches, most mangrove forests completely recover from storm damage within a year's time.

Mangrove forests are also important to their ecosystems due to the amount of biological diversity found within them. In the water, shrimp, crabs, and lobsters frequently make their homes on the seafloor in mangrove forests. There are many animals that cling to the roots of mangroves; among them are oysters, anemones, snails, and worms. The roots also provide havens for fish to hide from predators, so large numbers of fish species lay their eggs in mangrove forests. The fish often remain in the root systems from the time they hatch until they grow large enough to brave the open ocean waters. For instance, some species of groupers remain in the waters of mangrove forests for several years until they reach a meter or so in length and then depart for coral reefs.

Above the water, all kinds of mammals, birds, amphibians, insects, and reptiles make their homes in mangrove forests. Biologists estimate that more than 340 threatened or endangered species make their homes in mangrove forests. Included in this group are Bengal tigers, dugongs, red colobus monkeys, and sambar deer. Other types of animals, such as numerous species of primates and birds, both migratory and those that live in mangrove forests all year long, can be found in them as well. So can many endangered and threatened trees, bushes, and flowers. Fortunately, efforts are being made to preserve mangrove forests in countries around the world, so it is likely that these endangered species, both animals and plants, will see their numbers recover in the near future.

Glossary

brackish: slightly salty; containing both fresh and salt water
osmosis: the process of absorption

Mangrove Forests

¹ → Few trees are able to survive in **brackish** water, yet the approximately eighty species of mangrove trees thrive in this kind of environment. Mangroves are typically found growing along coastlines in tropical and subtropical conditions. These trees grow closely together, and their roots, many of which grow aboveground, combine to form thick tangles referred to as mangrove forests. Mangrove forests are extremely vital to their local environments for a number of reasons.

1 In paragraph 1, the author implies that mangrove trees

Ⓐ do not grow tall because they grow so closely together
Ⓑ require hot or warm weather in order to grow well
Ⓒ prevent other trees from growing anywhere near them
Ⓓ are important sources of lumber for local residents

📖 *Glossary*

brackish: slightly salty; containing both fresh and salt water

2 → Due to the diversity of mangrove species, some may only grow around 1.5 meters in height, making them shrubs, whereas others may rise forty meters or more high. Despite these differences in size, all mangroves share the ability to live in salty water and low oxygen conditions. One adaptation that permits mangroves to thrive is that they have defenses protecting them from salt in water. Some, called non-secreters, create barriers that prevent salt from being absorbed through the process of **osmosis**, which is how they take in water. Other mangroves, known as secreters, take in salt along with the water they absorb but then undergo a process to remove the salt through pores or salt glands located in their leaves. This capability permits some mangroves to grow in water containing two times the salt content of the ocean.

2 Select the TWO answer choices from paragraph 2 that identify characteristics of mangrove trees. *To receive credit, you must select TWO answers.*

Ⓐ They must absorb some salt in order to survive.
Ⓑ They can grow in water that is saltier than the ocean.
Ⓒ They are able to grow in soil that has little oxygen.
Ⓓ They are capable of removing salt through their branches.

3 The author discusses "secreters" in paragraph 2 in order to

Ⓐ compare their defenses against salt with those of non-secreters
Ⓑ point out that the majority of mangrove trees are secreters
Ⓒ explain the process of how they remove salt in detail
Ⓓ describe how they manage to absorb oxygen from the soil

📖 *Glossary*

osmosis: the process of absorption

³ ➜ A second adaptation that benefits mangroves is root aeration, which enables them to survive in soil without oxygen. While mangroves undergo photosynthesis to create energy for themselves, they still require oxygen for their cells. Most trees simply absorb oxygen from gases found in the soil, but because mangrove roots are flooded with water, they have undergone adaptations to enable them to access oxygen. Some mangroves have aboveground roots that rise above the water level and therefore enable the plant to obtain oxygen from the air. Some of these roots, which can be quite high, keep the trunks of mangroves entirely above water while also providing stability for the trees.

4. Which of the sentences below best expresses the essential information in the highlighted sentence in the passage? *Incorrect* answer choices change the meaning in important ways or leave out essential information.
   - (A) Mangrove roots have changed to get access to oxygen since they are flooded by water and cannot take in oxygen in the soil like most trees.
   - (B) Many trees can absorb oxygen that is in the soil, but mangrove trees cannot do that because they are always covered by water.
   - (C) When mangroves grow in watery conditions, they need to adapt themselves so that their roots are capable of absorbing water.
   - (D) The majority of trees have adapted to being flooded with water, but mangrove trees have roots that cannot give them access to oxygen.

5. According to paragraph 3, which of the following is true of mangrove roots?
   - (A) They provide more support for their trees than the trunk does.
   - (B) They can sometimes prevent water from touching the trunks of their trees.
   - (C) They almost always grow above the ground instead of in the soil.
   - (D) They are better able to extract nutrients from water than from the ground.

Most mangroves grow between twenty-five degrees latitude north and twenty-five degrees latitude south, which is the area close to the equator. There are vast expanses of mangrove forests on the coasts of Central and South America, Africa, the Middle East, India, Southeast Asia, and Australia. These are all places which see frequent tropical storms such as hurricanes, typhoons, and cyclones. When powerful tropical storms—and also tsunamis caused by undersea earthquakes—send storm surges toward shore, mangrove forests are effective at mitigating their effects. The facts that the trees grow closely together and have complex aboveground root structures help reduce the sizes of waves approaching the shore. While strong winds may knock some trees over and break off branches, most mangrove forests completely recover from storm damage within a year's time.

6. The word "mitigating" in the passage is closest in meaning to
   Ⓐ enhancing
   Ⓑ withstanding
   Ⓒ fighting
   Ⓓ reducing

5 → Mangrove forests are also important to their ecosystems due to the amount of biological diversity found within them. In the water, shrimp, crabs, and lobsters frequently make their homes on the seafloor in mangrove forests. There are many animals that cling to the roots of mangroves; among them are oysters, anemones, snails, and worms. The roots also provide havens for fish to hide from predators, so large numbers of fish species lay their eggs in mangrove forests. The fish often remain in the root systems from the time they hatch until they grow large enough to brave the open ocean waters. For instance, some species of groupers remain in the waters of mangrove forests for several years until they reach a meter or so in length and then depart for coral reefs.

7. In paragraph 5, the author uses "shrimp, crabs, and lobsters" as examples of

Ⓐ creatures that depart mangrove forests when they get older
Ⓑ animals that hide from predators in mangrove forests
Ⓒ creatures that live in the water beneath mangrove trees
Ⓓ animals that live by clinging to the roots of mangrove trees

6 → Above the water, all kinds of mammals, birds, amphibians, insects, and reptiles make their homes in mangrove forests. Biologists estimate that more than 340 threatened or endangered species make their homes in mangrove forests. Included in this group are Bengal tigers, dugongs, red colobus monkeys, and sambar deer. Other types of animals, such as numerous species of primates and birds, both migratory and those that live in mangrove forests all year long, can be found in them as well. So can many endangered and threatened trees, bushes, and flowers. Fortunately, efforts are being made to preserve mangrove forests in countries around the world, so it is likely that these endangered species, both animals and plants, will see their numbers recover in the near future.

8. In paragraph 6, all of the following questions are answered EXCEPT:

Ⓐ What are some endangered or threatened animals living in mangrove forests?

Ⓑ What is the expected future for endangered species in mangrove forests?

Ⓒ What are some different types of animals found in mangrove forests?

Ⓓ Which mangrove forests have the most endangered species living in them?

Most mangroves grow between twenty-five degrees latitude north and twenty-five degrees latitude south, which is the area close to the equator. There are vast expanses of mangrove forests on the coasts of Central and South America, Africa, the Middle East, India, Southeast Asia, and Australia. These are all places which see frequent tropical storms such as hurricanes, typhoons, and cyclones. ■ When powerful tropical storms—and also tsunamis caused by undersea earthquakes—send storm surges toward shore, mangrove forests are effective at mitigating their effects. ■ The facts that the trees grow closely together and have complex aboveground root structures help reduce the sizes of waves approaching the shore. ■ While strong winds may knock some trees over and break off branches, most mangrove forests completely recover from storm damage within a year's time. ■

9. Look at the four squares [■] that indicate where the following sentence could be added to the passage.

The result is that areas on land located behind mangrove forests suffer less flooding than other places do.

Where would the sentence best fit?

Click on a square [■] to add the sentence to the passage.

10 Directions: An introductory sentence for a brief summary of the passage is provided below. Complete the summary by selecting the THREE answer choices that express the most important ideas of the passage. Some sentences do not belong because they express ideas that are not presented in the passage or are minor ideas in the passage. **This question is worth 2 points.**

Drag your answer choices to the spaces where they belong.
To remove an answer choice, click on it. To review the passage, click on **View Text**.

Mangrove forests are of great importance to their ecosystems for several reasons.

-
-
-

Answer Choices

1. Non-secreters are more common mangrove trees than secreter mangrove trees.
2. Many animals live both in the water under mangrove trees and in the trees themselves.
3. There are many species of mangrove trees that can be both short and very tall.
4. Mangrove forests are capable of reducing the power of storm surges and tsunamis.
5. Numerous endangered plants and animals make their homes in mangrove forests.
6. The roots of some mangrove trees grow high above the ground and do not touch the water.

Alternative Therapy

As healthcare costs continually rise in most developed countries, many people are looking to alternative forms of health therapy both to prevent various illnesses and to cure them of their problems. Two of the most popular forms of alternative therapies in the West today are acupuncture and herbal medicine, both of which have been used in Asia for centuries and are rooted in ancient Chinese medicine. In essence, they attempt to treat the source of the health problem rather than simply get rid of the symptoms, which is something that many argue is the flawed crux of Western medicinal techniques. For this reason, many individuals are taking a more holistic approach to their bodies and health rather than simply looking for quick cures. For example, instead of taking aspirin whenever they get headaches, some people go to an acupuncturist to find out what is causing the problem and begin treatments for that specific cause, which will prevent the headaches from returning in the future. In this way, alternative medicine such as acupuncture and herbal therapy have wonderful preventative potential many modern medicines do not.

Acupuncture is based on ancient Chinese medicine and the importance of *ki*, a kind of life force that **pulsates** through every human's body. *Ki* runs through various pathways in the body and is fundamental in giving humans strength and energy as well as bolstering the immune system. But at times, these pathways might suffer blockage or be disrupted for various reasons, so *ki* is unable to flow smoothly through the body. When this occurs, the body becomes vulnerable to illness and pain. This is when acupuncture can be of assistance. Acupuncturists are well versed in the mapping of the *ki* pathways throughout the body and are able to locate and stimulate certain areas on the surface of the body in order to relieve the pressure and to allow *ki* once more to flow freely, eliminating pains and illnesses in the process.

One of the most common and successful methods of acupuncture is described as ear acupuncture. As its name implies, this technique is involved solely with the ear and its numerous activation points. The ear is considered a highly sensitive area of the human body because it contains a strong, healthy flow of blood as well as numerous nerve points that connect it with the rest of the human body. Acupuncturists place tiny needles in the surface of the skin at certain points, depending on the desired result. In general, ear acupuncture is considered an excellent therapy, especially for treating individuals with psychological or physical dependency issues such as eating disorders and drug or alcohol abuse.

A second form of alternative therapy based on Chinese traditional medicine is herbal therapy, a process in which special herbs are prescribed by a doctor to be taken in a hot liquid form, usually tea. Traditionally, herbal teas are **imbibed** to boost the immune system and to prevent illnesses from being able to enter the body. Herbs also have a more immediate influence than acupuncture on the body's physical systems, such as the circulatory system, as they can assist in normalizing blood pressure. One excellent example of an herbal remedy is mushroom tea, which is an excellent antioxidant. Other benefits attributed to the use of traditional Chinese herbs are that they build stamina and are good for digestive purposes. Sometimes herbal medicines are used in conjunction with acupuncture to magnify its effects.

When it comes to diseases and preventative measures, people should realize that there are many proven alternatives simply to visiting a local Western doctor or hospital to be evaluated and sent home with various prescriptions. In many cases, this type of medicine only masks the essence of the problem while traditional Chinese therapy such as acupuncture and herbal medicine addresses it from the onset. As the popularity of alternative therapies such as these grows, hopefully, more and more individuals will seek them out and benefit from their holistic approaches. Ultimately, alternative therapies such as herbs or acupuncture can work wonders as preventative methods for physiological as well as psychological problems before they are able to manifest symptoms and cause pain and suffering.

Glossary
pulsate: to expand and contract rhythmically
imbibe: to drink something

Alternative Therapy

1 → As healthcare costs continually rise in most developed countries, many people are looking to alternative forms of health therapy both to prevent various illnesses and to cure them of their problems. Two of the most popular forms of alternative therapies in the West today are acupuncture and herbal medicine, both of which have been used in Asia for centuries and are rooted in ancient Chinese medicine. In essence, they attempt to treat the source of the health problem rather than simply get rid of the symptoms, which is something that many argue is the flawed crux of Western medicinal techniques. For this reason, many individuals are taking a more holistic approach to their bodies and health rather than simply looking for quick cures. For example, instead of taking aspirin whenever they get headaches, some people go to an acupuncturist to find out what is causing the problem and begin treatments for that specific cause, which will prevent the headaches from returning in the future. In this way, alternative medicine such as acupuncture and herbal therapy have wonderful preventative potential many modern medicines do not.

11 The word "crux" in the passage is closest in meaning to
- Ⓐ application
- Ⓑ relief
- Ⓒ symptom
- Ⓓ basis

12 The author discusses "headaches" in paragraph 1 in order to
- Ⓐ show how they are one of the most common ailments for humans
- Ⓑ question whether they can be cured with traditional medicine
- Ⓒ note that they reveal deeper problems inside human bodies
- Ⓓ indicate aspirin is still the best remedy for this type of problem

13 Which of the following can be inferred from paragraph 1 about acupuncture?
- Ⓐ It has been in constant use by herbalists for hundreds of years in the Orient.
- Ⓑ Its focus is more intrinsic as opposed to the extrinsic methods of Western medicine.
- Ⓒ Its benefits accrue over a longer period of time than those of other therapies.
- Ⓓ It attempts to treat both the symptoms and the source of a patient's illness.

2 → Acupuncture is based on ancient Chinese medicine and the importance of *ki*, a kind of life force that **pulsates** through every human's body. *Ki* runs through various pathways in the body and is fundamental in giving humans strength and energy as well as bolstering the immune system. But at times, these pathways might suffer blockage or be disrupted for various reasons, so *ki* is unable to flow smoothly through the body. When this occurs, the body becomes vulnerable to illness and pain. This is when acupuncture can be of assistance. **Acupuncturists are well versed in the mapping of the *ki* pathways throughout the body and are able to locate and stimulate certain areas on the surface of the body in order to relieve the pressure and to allow *ki* once more to flow freely, eliminating pains and illnesses in the process.**

14. Which of the sentences below best expresses the essential information in the highlighted sentence in the passage? *Incorrect* answer choices change the meaning in important ways or leave out essential information.

    A. *Ki* paths are opened when they stimulate parts of the body and relieve pressure on painful areas with the assistance of professional acupuncturists.
    B. Acupuncturists are knowledgeable in the pathways of *ki*, so they make use of this knowledge to find out what areas of the body to place needles in.
    C. The expertise of acupuncturists allows them to free up *ki* pathways in the body and to help the patient recover from his sickness.
    D. Illnesses and pain are relieved once the acupuncturist is able to map the pathways of *ki* and discover the source of the pressure.

15. According to paragraph 2, which of the following is true of *ki*?

    A. It constantly runs through the various blood vessels of the body.
    B. It is the basis upon which the method of acupuncture was devised.
    C. It is an invisible force that blocks the pathways of the body.
    D. It stimulates certain pathways in the body and relieves pain.

Glossary

pulsate: to expand and contract rhythmically

3 → One of the most common and successful methods of acupuncture is described as ear acupuncture. As its name implies, this technique is involved solely with the ear and its numerous activation points. The ear is considered a highly sensitive area of the human body because it contains a strong, healthy flow of blood as well as numerous nerve points that connect it with the rest of the human body. Acupuncturists place tiny needles in the surface of the skin at certain points, depending on the desired result. In general, ear acupuncture is considered an excellent therapy, especially for treating individuals with psychological or physical dependency issues such as eating disorders and drug or alcohol abuse.

16. According to paragraph 3, which of the following is true of the ear?

Ⓐ It contains a small number of the body's special activation points.

Ⓑ It has a healthy blood supply, which relieves pain people get from needles.

Ⓒ It is a beneficial acupuncture area because it contains plenty of nerves.

Ⓓ It is the source of dependency issues such as alcoholism and drug use.

⁴ ➜ A second form of alternative therapy based on Chinese traditional medicine is herbal therapy, a process in which special herbs are prescribed by a doctor to be taken in a hot liquid form, usually tea. Traditionally, herbal teas are **imbibed** to boost the immune system and to prevent illnesses from being able to enter the body. Herbs also have a more immediate influence than acupuncture on the body's physical systems, such as the circulatory system, as they can assist in normalizing blood pressure. One excellent example of an herbal remedy is mushroom tea, which is an excellent antioxidant. Other benefits attributed to the use of traditional Chinese herbs are that they build stamina and are good for digestive purposes. Sometimes herbal medicines are used in conjunction with acupuncture to magnify its effects.

17 According to paragraph 4, which of the following is NOT true of herbal therapy?

(A) Herbs are an excellent way of increasing a person's endurance.

(B) It is used as a preventative form of therapy for healthy people.

(C) It is normally taken by people in the form of various pills.

(D) It is beneficial to the circulatory system and blood pressure problems.

📖 Glossary
imbibe: to drink something

5 → When it comes to diseases and preventative measures, people should realize that there are many proven alternatives simply to visiting a local Western doctor or hospital to be evaluated and sent home with various prescriptions. ■ In many cases, this type of medicine only masks the essence of the problem while traditional Chinese therapy such as acupuncture and herbal medicine addresses it from the onset. ■ As the popularity of alternative therapies such as these grows, hopefully, more and more individuals will seek them out and benefit from their holistic approaches. ■ Ultimately, alternative therapies such as herbs or acupuncture can work wonders as preventative methods for physiological as well as psychological problems before they are able to manifest symptoms and cause pain and suffering. ■

18. Which of the following can be inferred from paragraph 5 about Western doctors' prescriptions?
   Ⓐ They are too expensive for many people to afford.
   Ⓑ They may only address one level of various illnesses.
   Ⓒ They are fundamental to most alternative therapies.
   Ⓓ They enable patients to get back on their feet rapidly.

19. Look at the four squares [■] that indicate where the following sentence could be added to the passage.

   Additionally, some illnesses require much more investigation than this.

   Where would the sentence best fit?

   Click on a square [■] to add the sentence to the passage.

20 **Directions:** An introductory sentence for a brief summary of the passage is provided below. Complete the summary by selecting the THREE answer choices that express the most important ideas of the passage. Some sentences do not belong because they express ideas that are not presented in the passage or are minor ideas in the passage. **This question is worth 2 points.**

Drag your answer choices to the spaces where they belong.
To remove an answer choice, click on it. To review the passage, click on **View Text**.

People in many developed countries are turning away from Western medicine and seeking alternative forms of treatment.

-
-
-

Answer Choices

1. Traditional therapies seek to deal with the actual problem rather than to get rid of the symptoms.
2. Western medicine often ignores the reasons why people actually become sick.
3. Herbal therapies, such as drinking tea, can assist in improving the immune system.
4. The cost of health care has been rising rapidly in many Western countries.
5. People have been using traditional therapies from Asia for thousands of years.
6. Acupuncture involves using needles to help the flow of *ki*, a life force in the body.

How to Master Skills for the TOEFL iBT

Actual Test
READING 1

04

TOEFL READING

Reading Section Directions

This section measures your ability to understand academic passages in English. You will have **35 minutes** to read and answer questions about **2 passages**. A clock at the top of the screen will show you how much time is remaining.

Most questions are worth 1 point but the last question for each passage is worth more than 1 point. The directions for the last question indicate how many points you may receive.

Some passages include a word or phrase that is **underlined** in blue. Click on the word or phrase to see a definition or an explanation.

When you want to move to the next question, click on **Next**. You may skip questions and go back to them later. If you want to return to previous questions, click on **Back**. You can click on **Review** at any time, and the review screen will show you which questions you have answered and which you have not answered. From this review screen, you may go directly to any question you have already seen in the Reading section.

Click on **Continue** to go on.

A Change of Orbit

Earth has sustained life for millions of years, yet the other planets in our solar system are incapable of doing so. This is primarily the result of the unique position Earth occupies in the solar system, as it is neither too close nor too far from the sun to upset the delicate temperature requirements of life. Our position is in what astronomers call the habitable zone, the place where life exists. Yet if Earth's orbit around the sun were thrown off by just a few degrees, all life on the planet could be in danger. Such an event could happen if a passing massive gravitation field influenced Earth's orbit. Astronomers have experimented extensively with such possibilities and have reached a surprising conclusion: Earth could sustain life if its orbit were changed in minor ways but only with a great **dislocation** of life.

Astronomers define the habitable zone as the region seventy-five to 140 million miles from a star with the intensity of our sun. Venus and Mars are outside this zone, the former too close to the sun and the latter too far away. Earth's orbit is a near perfect circle, almost always ninety-three million miles from the sun. The average temperature of the Earth is fifty-eight degrees Fahrenheit with average highs of 107°F and lows of -81°F. The axis is tilted so that Earth has various seasons at the northern and southern regions with the equatorial regions having similar weather all year round.

The great fear is that a passing black hole will influence Earth's orbit. Black holes are areas of massive gravitational energy that devour all things they encounter, including stars. Astronomers have created computer modeling that allows them to run different orbits for Earth and examined the influences they would have on temperature and climate. As a control element, the computer model maintained Earth's orbital period of 365 days. Minor variations in the orbit would keep Earth inside the habitable zone all year while a great shift would have Earth passing closer to the sun than Mercury on one end and being beyond the orbit of Mars on the other. Such large changes would dramatically change the climate.

The amazing revelation the astronomers discovered was that with orbital changes in the midrange, life was still possible, but there would be significant changes in human places of habitation. Water, which around three-fourths of the planet's surface is covered with, has a tremendous capacity to retain heat. As Earth came extremely close to the sun, the water would pick up massive amounts of heat, which would be used to maintain livable temperature as Earth moved out to the colder regions near Mars. With an orbit passing near Venus but not beyond Mars, temperatures would average seventy-three degrees Fahrenheit, which is very livable. However, there would be great changes for the inhabitants of different parts of the globe. People at the equator would suffer temperatures above 140°F at times, and rivers and lakes would evaporate. The polar ice caps would melt, and the coastlines would change, drowning coastal cities. Northern Canada and Russia would become prime real estate, even during the period when Earth's orbit was near Mars as the heat absorbed by the oceans would maintain a livable temperature and forestall the return of the ice caps to a great degree.

At the other extreme, with Earth inside Mercury's orbit and outside Mars's, the temperatures would make life impossible in much of the world, especially the equatorial regions. In a scenario where Earth was closest to the sun in March and April and farthest away in October and November, the temperatures in Africa, India, South America, and Australia would reach almost 200°F, near water's boiling point, in March. These areas would cool down by October, but it is highly unlikely that people would form permanent living centers there as the great heat would return in March. **The bottom line** is that Earth will remain livable if its orbit changes mainly because of the great resources of heat-absorbing water. However, this would only happen because we would still pass close to the sun at one point. If Earth had an orbit permanently outside the habitable zone, either too close or far away from the sun, most life would surely perish.

Glossary
dislocation: a displacement; disruption
the bottom line: the most important thing; the essential point

A Change of Orbit

Earth has sustained life for millions of years, yet the other planets in our solar system are incapable of doing so. This is primarily the result of the unique position Earth occupies in the solar system, as it is neither too close nor too far from the sun to upset the delicate temperature requirements of life. Our position is in what astronomers call the habitable zone, the place where life exists. Yet if Earth's orbit around the sun were thrown off by just a few degrees, all life on the planet could be in danger. Such an event could happen if a passing massive gravitation field influenced Earth's orbit. Astronomers have experimented extensively with such possibilities and have reached a surprising conclusion: Earth could sustain life if its orbit were changed in minor ways but only with a great **dislocation** of life.

1. The word "delicate" in the passage is closest in meaning to
   - Ⓐ subtle
   - Ⓑ fragile
   - Ⓒ considerate
   - Ⓓ graceful

📖 Glossary

dislocation: a displacement; disruption

2 → Astronomers define the habitable zone as the region seventy-five to 140 million miles from a star with the intensity of our sun. Venus and Mars are outside this zone, the former too close to the sun and the latter too far away. Earth's orbit is a near perfect circle, almost always ninety-three million miles from the sun. The average temperature of the Earth is fifty-eight degrees Fahrenheit with average highs of 107°F and lows of -81°F. The axis is tilted so that Earth has various seasons at the northern and southern regions with the equatorial regions having similar weather all year round.

2. According to paragraph 2, all of the following factors influence the climate on Earth EXCEPT:

(A) Earth's nearly symmetrical orbit around the sun

(B) the angle of Earth's axis as it rotates

(C) Earth's position between two other planets

(D) Earth's average distance from the sun

³ ⟶ The great fear is that a passing black hole will influence Earth's orbit. Black holes are areas of massive gravitational energy that devour all things they encounter, including stars. Astronomers have created computer modeling that allows them to run different orbits for Earth and examined the influences they would have on temperature and climate. As a control element, the computer model maintained Earth's orbital period of 365 days. Minor variations in the orbit would keep Earth inside the habitable zone all year while a great shift would have Earth passing closer to the sun than Mercury on one end and being beyond the orbit of Mars on the other. Such large changes would dramatically change the climate.

3 The word "they" in the passage refers to
- Ⓐ black holes
- Ⓑ stars
- Ⓒ astronomers
- Ⓓ different orbits

4 According to paragraph 3, astronomers kept Earth's orbital period the same in their experiments in order to
- Ⓐ judge which months on the planet would be hot and which ones cold
- Ⓑ maintain a familiar element as a reference point for their assessment
- Ⓒ prove that the orbital period would not alter with a change in orbits
- Ⓓ demonstrate that a change in orbits would cause a change in seasons

4 → The amazing revelation the astronomers discovered was that with orbital changes in the midrange, life was still possible, but there would be significant changes in human places of habitation. Water, which around three-fourths of the planet's surface is covered with, has a tremendous capacity to retain heat. As Earth came extremely close to the sun, the water would pick up massive amounts of heat, which would be used to maintain livable temperature as Earth moved out to the colder regions near Mars. With an orbit passing near Venus but not beyond Mars, temperatures would average seventy-three degrees Fahrenheit, which is very livable. However, there would be great changes for the inhabitants of different parts of the globe. People at the equator would suffer temperatures above 140°F at times, and rivers and lakes would evaporate. The polar ice caps would melt, and the coastlines would change, drowning coastal cities. Northern Canada and Russia would become prime real estate, even during the period when Earth's orbit was near Mars as the heat absorbed by the oceans would maintain a livable temperature and forestall the return of the ice caps to a great degree.

5. Which of the sentences below best expresses the essential information in the highlighted sentence in the passage? *Incorrect* answer choices change the meaning in important ways or leave out essential information.

    (A) It was surprising for the astronomers to discover that with orbital shifts in the midrange, Earth could still sustain life with no significant changes.
    (B) Not surprisingly, the astronomers found out that with mild orbital changes, life was still possible on Earth, but human beings would go extinct.
    (C) Surprisingly, the astronomers learned that with mid-range orbital changes, people could not live in the same places even though Earth could still sustain life.
    (D) If Earth's orbit changed in the midrange, people could not live in the same places on Earth, which surprised the astronomers.

6. The word "forestall" in the passage is closest in meaning to
    (A) warn
    (B) anticipate
    (C) cause
    (D) prevent

⁵→ At the other extreme, with Earth inside Mercury's orbit and outside Mars's, the temperatures would make life impossible in much of the world, especially the equatorial regions. In a scenario where Earth was closest to the sun in March and April and farthest away in October and November, the temperatures in Africa, India, South America, and Australia would reach almost 200°F, near water's boiling point, in March. These areas would cool down by October, but it is highly unlikely that people would form permanent living centers there as the great heat would return in March. **The bottom line** is that Earth will remain livable if its orbit changes mainly because of the great resources of heat-absorbing water. However, this would only happen because we would still pass close to the sun at one point. If Earth had an orbit permanently outside the habitable zone, either too close or far away from the sun, most life would surely perish.

7. It can be inferred from paragraphs 4 and 5 that after a mild shift in Earth's orbit, most humans would
   Ⓐ live in the planet's northern regions
   Ⓑ live on water near the coastal areas
   Ⓒ remain living where they are now
   Ⓓ move to the interiors of the continents

8. According to paragraph 5, people would be unlikely to maintain permanent habitats in the equatorial regions in an orbit inside Mercury because of
   Ⓐ the extremes in temperatures during the different seasons
   Ⓑ the great amounts of water that would be lost in the summertime
   Ⓒ the extreme heat in summer that would kill any creatures there
   Ⓓ the constant migrations that people living there would make

📖 Glossary

the bottom line: the most important thing; the essential point

■ At the other extreme, with Earth inside Mercury's orbit and outside Mars's, the temperatures would make life impossible in much of the world, especially the equatorial regions. ■ In a scenario where Earth was closest to the sun in March and April and farthest away in October and November, the temperatures in Africa, India, South America, and Australia would reach almost 200°F, near water's boiling point, in March. ■ These areas would cool down by October, but it is highly unlikely that people would form permanent living centers there as the great heat would return in March. ■ **The bottom line** is that Earth will remain livable if its orbit changes mainly because of the great resources of heat-absorbing water. However, this would only happen because we would still pass close to the sun at one point. If Earth had an orbit permanently outside the habitable zone, either too close or far away from the sun, most life would surely perish.

Glossary

the bottom line: the most important thing; the essential point

---

9. Look at the four squares [■] that indicate where the following sentence could be added to the passage.

   One of the big questions, which had no concrete answer, was in which months Earth would be closest to and farthest from the sun.

   Where would the sentence best fit?

   Click on a square [■] to add the sentence to the passage.

10 Directions: An introductory sentence for a brief summary of the passage is provided below. Complete the summary by selecting the THREE answer choices that express the most important ideas of the passage. Some sentences do not belong because they express ideas that are not presented in the passage or are minor ideas in the passage. **This question is worth 2 points.**

Drag your answer choices to the spaces where they belong.
To remove an answer choice, click on it. To review the passage, click on **View Text**.

Alterations to Earth's orbit would cause various changes in conditions on the planet.

-
-
-

Answer Choices

1. Most of Earth's water would evaporate if it orbited the sun close to Mercury.

2. Small orbital changes keeping Earth in the habitable zone would result in minor temperature changes.

3. Astronomers believe that a black hole is causing changes in Earth's orbit right now.

4. Water would have a major effect on keeping Earth livable if its orbit changed.

5. Orbital changes taking Earth close to Mercury or Mars would make parts of the planet unlivable.

6. The temperature on Earth might rise a few degrees with a slight change in the planet's orbit.

The Influence of the Nile River on Egyptian Civilization

Philae Temple on an island in the Nile

The Nile River flows northward more than 4,100 miles from central Africa and completes its lengthy journey at the Mediterranean Sea. On the final leg of its trip, it travels through Egypt, where it is surrounded by the Sahara Desert. Ancient Egypt was one of the earliest human civilizations to arise. Without the Nile, ancient Egypt never would have existed, for the river had a tremendous effect on Egyptian civilization in a number of ways, including providing food for the Egyptian populace, being used as a method of transportation, and creating an identity for the Egyptian people themselves.

The primary manner in which the Nile River influenced Egyptian civilization is that it enabled a large population of people to live in one of the world's hottest, driest deserts. Every year in late summer, rising water levels caused the Nile River to flood. The waters of the Nile carried dark, fertile sediment when they overflowed the riverbanks, and they deposited this soil on the land. The Egyptians planted crops such as wheat, barley, and flax in the soil, which transformed parts of the desert into productive farmland and permitted farmers to grow enough food for the Egyptian people. The Egyptians also developed a system of irrigation canals allowing them to provide water for the crops in their fields. For instance, the Egyptians captured large amounts of floodwaters in manmade ponds and ditches they constructed. When the floodwaters receded, the farmers still retained water, which they used to help their plants grow. The flooding of the Nile was so important to the Egyptians that they based one of their calendars on it. The Egyptian new year was therefore considered to start with the advent of the flood season.

Another important aspect of the Nile River was that the Egyptians used it for transportation. Over the centuries, the Egyptians became master shipbuilders who constructed both small ships that were essentially rafts and larger ones that could be sailed by using either oars or sails. The Egyptians utilized papyrus to make small boats and rafts but also used wood, a rare raw material in the desert land, for larger ones. They employed boats for fishing as well as to transport food from place to place while people additionally sailed up and down the Nile to reach different places. The stone blocks that were used to construct the pyramids were dug out of **quarries** and then transported up or down the Nile to wherever they were needed.

Over time, ships became such an important part of Egyptian culture that they assumed a vital position in Egyptian mythology. For instance, the sun god, Ra, sailed across the heavens in a boat each day. An alabaster boat was found in the tomb of King Tutankhamun when it was discovered by Howard Carter. Other pharaohs were buried with boats or ships that were sturdy enough to have sailed on the Nile itself. The **Barque** of Amum was maintained at Thebes. It was covered in gold and was decorated with all kinds of ornaments. It—and other ships constructed by the Egyptians—was used for various festivals, which shows the importance of the Nile to Egyptian culture.

The Nile even contributed to forging the identity of the Egyptian people. The Egyptians recognized the lifegiving powers of the river's waters, so they held numerous festivals and rituals to honor the Nile. Many ancient Egyptian works of architecture, including temples and tombs, were constructed near the Nile as well. Various Egyptian religious beliefs were additionally associated with the Nile. Osiris, one of the most powerful gods in the Egyptian pantheon, was said to have been the deity who taught the Egyptian people how to farm the land. Hapi was the Egyptian god of the Nile. He was also a fertility god, which shows how the Egyptians associated the river with life. The Egyptians even divided the land on which they lived into Kemet, the black land, and Deshret, the dry land. Kemet was the land found in the Nile River Valley that was fertile and could sustain both people and agriculture. Deshret, on the other hand, was the hot, dry desert land, which only brought chaos and death to people.

Glossary
quarry: a place where people dig for stones such as limestone or marble
barque: a small sailing ship

The Influence of the Nile River on Egyptian Civilization

1 → The Nile River flows northward more than 4,100 miles from central Africa and completes its lengthy journey at the Mediterranean Sea. On the final leg of its trip, it travels through Egypt, where it is surrounded by the Sahara Desert. Ancient Egypt was one of the earliest human civilizations to arise. Without the Nile, ancient Egypt never would have existed, for the river had a tremendous effect on Egyptian civilization in a number of ways, including providing food for the Egyptian populace, being used as a method of transportation, and creating an identity for the Egyptian people themselves.

11 In paragraph 1, the author uses "the Sahara Desert" as an example of

Ⓐ a lifeless land despite the presence of the Nile River
Ⓑ a place where few people in Egypt ever venture
Ⓒ a geographical feature found adjacent to the Nile River
Ⓓ a large desert that has extremely hot temperatures

12 In paragraph 1, all of the following questions are answered EXCEPT:

Ⓐ What is true about the ancient Egyptian civilization around the Nile River?
Ⓑ In what ways was the Nile River important to ancient Egypt?
Ⓒ How long does it take the Nile River to flow to the sea?
Ⓓ What are the starting and ending points of the Nile River?

The primary manner in which the Nile River influenced Egyptian civilization is that it enabled a large population of people to live in one of the world's hottest, driest deserts. Every year in late summer, rising water levels caused the Nile River to flood. The waters of the Nile carried dark, fertile sediment when they overflowed the riverbanks, and they deposited this soil on the land. The Egyptians planted crops such as wheat, barley, and flax in the soil, which transformed parts of the desert into productive farmland and permitted farmers to grow enough food for the Egyptian people. The Egyptians also developed a system of irrigation canals allowing them to provide water for the crops in their fields. For instance, the Egyptians captured large amounts of floodwaters in manmade ponds and ditches they constructed. When the floodwaters receded, the farmers still retained water, which they used to help their plants grow. The flooding of the Nile was so important to the Egyptians that they based one of their calendars on it. The Egyptian new year was therefore considered to start with the advent of the flood season.

13 The word "they" in the passage refers to
  Ⓐ the world's hottest, driest deserts
  Ⓑ rising water levels
  Ⓒ the waters of the Nile
  Ⓓ the riverbanks

14 The word "receded" in the passage is closest in meaning to
  Ⓐ withdrew
  Ⓑ evaporated
  Ⓒ approached
  Ⓓ rose

³ ➡ Another important aspect of the Nile River was that the Egyptians used it for transportation. Over the centuries, the Egyptians became master shipbuilders who constructed both small ships that were essentially rafts and larger ones that could be sailed by using either oars or sails. The Egyptians utilized papyrus to make small boats and rafts but also used wood, a rare raw material in the desert land, for larger ones. They employed boats for fishing as well as to transport food from place to place while people additionally sailed up and down the Nile to reach different places. The stone blocks that were used to construct the pyramids were dug out of **quarries** and then transported up or down the Nile to wherever they were needed.

Glossary
quarry: a place where people dig for stones such as limestone or marble

15 Which of the sentences below best expresses the essential information in the highlighted sentence in the passage? *Incorrect* answer choices change the meaning in important ways or leave out essential information.

Ⓐ The Egyptians first made small rafts and then learned to make large sailing ships.

Ⓑ It was possible for the Egyptians to use rafts and sailing ships on the Nile River.

Ⓒ The Egyptians became skilled at making both large and small ships over time.

Ⓓ After hundreds of years, Egyptian shipbuilders learned the art of making various ships.

16 According to paragraph 3, which of the following is true of Egyptian ships?

Ⓐ They could sail up the Nile River as easily as they could sail down it.

Ⓑ They were used for the purposes of transporting both people and goods.

Ⓒ They were unable to transport heavy stones like those used in the pyramids.

Ⓓ They were all made with papyrus, which was easy to acquire in Egypt.

4 → Over time, ships became such an important part of Egyptian culture that they assumed a vital position in Egyptian mythology. For instance, the sun god, Ra, sailed across the heavens in a boat each day. An alabaster boat was found in the tomb of King Tutankhamun when it was discovered by Howard Carter. Other pharaohs were buried with boats or ships that were sturdy enough to have sailed on the Nile itself. The **Barque** of Amum was maintained at Thebes. It was covered in gold and was decorated with all kinds of ornaments. It—and other ships constructed by the Egyptians—was used for various festivals, which shows the importance of the Nile to Egyptian culture.

17 In paragraph 4, the author's description of the Barque of Amun mentions which of the following?

Ⓐ The year in which it was constructed
Ⓑ The material with which it was made
Ⓒ The manner in which it was utilized
Ⓓ The types of decorations that were on it

📖 *Glossary*
barque: a small sailing ship

⁵→ The Nile even contributed to forging the identity of the Egyptian people. The Egyptians recognized the lifegiving powers of the river's waters, so they held numerous festivals and rituals to honor the Nile. Many ancient Egyptian works of architecture, including temples and tombs, were constructed near the Nile as well. Various Egyptian religious beliefs were additionally associated with the Nile. Osiris, one of the most powerful gods in the Egyptian pantheon, was said to have been the deity who taught the Egyptian people how to farm the land. Hapi was the Egyptian god of the Nile. He was also a fertility god, which shows how the Egyptians associated the river with life. The Egyptians even divided the land on which they lived into Kemet, the black land, and Deshret, the dry land. Kemet was the land found in the Nile River Valley that was fertile and could sustain both people and agriculture. Deshret, on the other hand, was the hot, dry desert land, which only brought chaos and death to people.

18 In paragraph 5, the author implies that Deshret

Ⓐ contained some water in the form of wells and oases

Ⓑ was larger in size than the land that comprised Kemet

Ⓒ was capable of growing some crops for the Egyptian people

Ⓓ had few people living in it during the time of ancient Egypt

Over time, ships became such an important part of Egyptian culture that they assumed a vital position in Egyptian mythology. ■ For instance, the sun god, Ra, sailed across the heavens in a boat each day. ■ An alabaster boat was found in the tomb of King Tutankhamun when it was discovered by Howard Carter. ■ Other pharaohs were buried with boats or ships that were sturdy enough to have sailed on the Nile itself. ■ The **Barque** of Amum was maintained at Thebes. It was covered in gold and was decorated with all kinds of ornaments. It—and other ships constructed by the Egyptians—was used for various festivals, which shows the importance of the Nile to Egyptian culture.

19 Look at the four squares [■] that indicate where the following sentence could be added to the passage.

It is considered one of the most precious treasures from the pharaoh's hoard.

Where would the sentence best fit?

Click on a square [■] to add the sentence to the passage.

Glossary

barque: a small sailing ship

20 Directions: An introductory sentence for a brief summary of the passage is provided below. Complete the summary by selecting the THREE answer choices that express the most important ideas of the passage. Some sentences do not belong because they express ideas that are not presented in the passage or are minor ideas in the passage. **This question is worth 2 points.**

Drag your answer choices to the spaces where they belong.
To remove an answer choice, click on it. To review the passage, click on **View Text**.

The Nile River was vital to ancient Egyptian civilization.

-
-
-

Answer Choices

1. The Egyptians used boats to sail on the Nile and to transport various things.
2. Wheat, barley, and rice were some of the crops grown thanks to the Nile River.
3. The Egyptians believed in various gods, including Osiris and Hapi.
4. The flooding of the Nile brought fertile soil that was used to grow crops in.
5. There was a statue of a boat found in the tomb of King Tutankhamun.
6. Egyptian gods were connected to the Nile, and the river influenced local culture, too.

How to Master Skills for the TOEFL iBT

Actual Test
READING 1

05

TOEFL READING

Reading Section Directions

This section measures your ability to understand academic passages in English. You will have **35 minutes** to read and answer questions about **2 passages**. A clock at the top of the screen will show you how much time is remaining.

Most questions are worth 1 point but the last question for each passage is worth more than 1 point. The directions for the last question indicate how many points you may receive.

Some passages include a word or phrase that is **underlined** in blue. Click on the word or phrase to see a definition or an explanation.

When you want to move to the next question, click on **Next**. You may skip questions and go back to them later. If you want to return to previous questions, click on **Back**. You can click on **Review** at any time, and the review screen will show you which questions you have answered and which you have not answered. From this review screen, you may go directly to any question you have already seen in the Reading section.

Click on **Continue** to go on.

The Hydrogen Economy

Oil was in the depths of the planet for millions of years before humans found a use for it in the internal combustion engine. Unfortunately, this combination of resource and technology is so entrenched in people's way of life that it scarcely seems possible even to imagine a day when people may no longer be dependent on oil. One of the great fears is that the planet's supply of oil is finite and that the tank will one day run dry. In addition, oil and the pollutants it causes are choking life from the planet. However, the day when people no longer depend totally on oil may be in sight thanks to the recent development of the hydrogen fuel cell and practical applications for it.

The concept of the hydrogen fuel cell is quite simple: It is similar to a battery except that it contains oxygen and hydrogen in separate chambers. The electrons of the oxygen and the hydrogen are stripped away, leaving electricity and water as waste products. In fact, the space shuttle used hydrogen fuel cells to produce all of its electricity and water supplies and never had a problem. The quest for the hydrogen fuel cell began in the nineteenth century when Welshman Sir Robert Grove made the first documented one in history. Unfortunately, his subsequent hydrogen fuel cells never produced enough electricity to justify the expense of creating them. Not until the twentieth century was that problem solved. In 1959, the first vehicle, a tractor, was powered by hydrogen fuel. Yet the very few who knew about it viewed it as a novelty, so there was no great rush to produce more hydrogen vehicles.

Geoffrey Ballard, a Canadian engineer and environmentalist, is leading the charge to produce a hydrogen economy. His company, Ballard Power Systems, produced the first hydrogen cell-powered bus in 1993 and is at the **cutting edge** of hydrogen cell technology. It took Ballard a long time to reach this point since he had difficulty convincing his own managers and investors that he could make the bus. However, nothing breeds success like success, and once the bus was rolling, Ballard received interest and investment from several major automobile firms. Daimler-Benz produced the first hydrogen cell car in 1997.

4 → There are still many obstacles to overcome. One criticism of hydrogen-powered vehicles is that nobody will buy them because there is no easy source of hydrogen to replenish the supply. Hydrogen, although it is the most abundant element in the universe, is not freely found on Earth, meaning it is part of other elements such as oxygen, methane, natural gas, and even petroleum. Water contains a great deal of hydrogen and seems the best and cleanest source of hydrogen. However, separating hydrogen from oxygen requires the use of, ironically, electricity itself. Clean,

alternative means of making electricity such as with wind, water, and solar methods would justify the costs of separating the hydrogen. Ballard and his team have established another company called Hydrogen General to help develop the infrastructure of hydrogen separation and hydrogen supply points for future fleets of hydrogen-powered cars and buses. Several hydrogen stations have been established in Europe, and several countries are currently investing in future fleets of hydrogen-powered buses.

There has been some aid in this progress from various governments. California passed a bill in the late 1990s requiring ten percent of cars sold in that state to have zero-emissions of pollutants. With approximately forty million people, the largest population in the United States, this is a substantial number of cars. This law gave a boost to the manufacturing of hydrogen fuel celled cars by the big automobile makers. Despite these successes, there is still a long road ahead for the hydrogen economy. The world's infrastructure is run on oil and oil products. Massive expenditures would be required to transform our system to a hydrogen-based one, and many underdeveloped countries are unable to afford such a transformation. Finally, oil companies themselves are resisting the move with the specter of massive losses in revenue for decreasing oil sales staring them in the face. One day, people may no longer need oil, but that day is long off indeed.

Glossary

cutting edge: the most modern and advanced point in the development of something

The Hydrogen Economy

1 → Oil was in the depths of the planet for millions of years before humans found a use for it in the internal combustion engine. Unfortunately, this combination of resource and technology is so entrenched in people's way of life that it scarcely seems possible even to imagine a day when people may no longer be dependent on oil. One of the great fears is that the planet's supply of oil is finite and that the tank will one day run dry. In addition, oil and the pollutants it causes are choking life from the planet. However, the day when people no longer depend totally on oil may be in sight thanks to the recent development of the hydrogen fuel cell and practical applications for it.

1. According to paragraph 1, which of the following is NOT true of oil?
   Ⓐ People have an overly developed dependence on using it.
   Ⓑ People have replaced the use of oil with that of hydrogen.
   Ⓒ People may not be able to rely upon using it forever.
   Ⓓ It is a major cause of the world's environmental problems.

2 → The concept of the hydrogen fuel cell is quite simple: It is similar to a battery except that it contains oxygen and hydrogen in separate chambers. The electrons of the oxygen and the hydrogen are stripped away, leaving electricity and water as waste products. In fact, the space shuttle used hydrogen fuel cells to produce all of its electricity and water supplies and never had a problem. The quest for the hydrogen fuel cell began in the nineteenth century when Welshman Sir Robert Grove made the first documented one in history. Unfortunately, his subsequent hydrogen fuel cells never produced enough electricity to justify the expense of creating them. Not until the twentieth century was that problem solved. In 1959, the first vehicle, a tractor, was powered by hydrogen fuel. Yet the very few who knew about it viewed it as a novelty, so there was no great rush to produce more hydrogen vehicles.

2 In paragraph 2, the author mentions "the space shuttle used hydrogen fuel cells" in order to

- Ⓐ show that hydrogen fuel cells can be used in space
- Ⓑ prove that the space shuttle had the world's latest technology
- Ⓒ demonstrate that hydrogen fuel cells are reliable and safe
- Ⓓ explain how the space shuttle got all of its power

3 According to paragraph 2, it took a long time to develop practical hydrogen fuel cells because

- Ⓐ they were not cost efficient for people to construct
- Ⓑ there was no readily available source of hydrogen
- Ⓒ they produced too many waste products to dispose of
- Ⓓ no one was interested in either purchasing or using them

³→ Geoffrey Ballard, a Canadian engineer and environmentalist, is leading the charge to produce a hydrogen economy. His company, Ballard Power Systems, produced the first hydrogen cell-powered bus in 1993 and is at the **cutting edge** of hydrogen cell technology. It took Ballard a long time to reach this point since he had difficulty convincing his own managers and investors that he could make the bus. However, nothing breeds success like success, and once the bus was rolling, Ballard received interest and investment from several major automobile firms. Daimler-Benz produced the first hydrogen cell car in 1997.

4. According to paragraph 3, it took Geoffrey Ballard a long time to produce the first hydrogen-powered bus because

Ⓐ his invention was opposed by various automobile manufacturers
Ⓑ he lacked internal support and external investment for his idea
Ⓒ he had no way to make cheap hydrogen from his available resources
Ⓓ he was opposed by oil companies that did not want to lose profits

5. It can be inferred from paragraph 3 that automobile companies have invested in Ballard's company only because

Ⓐ he has the most experience of anyone with hydrogen power
Ⓑ they want to prevent his company from making hydrogen cars
Ⓒ they know that the world's oil supplies will run out someday
Ⓓ he has produced a practical use for the hydrogen fuel cell

📖 Glossary

cutting edge: the most modern and advanced point in the development of something

4 → There are still many obstacles to overcome. One criticism of hydrogen-powered vehicles is that nobody will buy them because there is no easy source of hydrogen to replenish the supply. Hydrogen, although it is the most abundant element in the universe, is not freely found on Earth, meaning it is part of other elements such as oxygen, methane, natural gas, and even petroleum. Water contains a great deal of hydrogen and seems the best and cleanest source of hydrogen. However, separating hydrogen from oxygen requires the use of, ironically, electricity itself. Clean, alternative means of making electricity such as with wind, water, and solar methods would justify the costs of separating the hydrogen. Ballard and his team have established another company called Hydrogen General to help develop the infrastructure of hydrogen separation and hydrogen supply points for future fleets of hydrogen-powered cars and buses. Several hydrogen stations have been established in Europe, and several countries are currently investing in future fleets of hydrogen-powered buses.

6. The word "replenish" in the passage is closest in meaning to
   A restock
   B revitalize
   C revive
   D reinforce

7. According to paragraph 4, Hydrogen General was created in order to
   A develop the foundation that countries require for a hydrogen economy
   B battle the people and companies opposed to the hydrogen economy
   C convince people of the need to take part in the hydrogen economy
   D find more sources of hydrogen that can be reproduced cheaply

There has been some aid in this progress from various governments. California passed a bill in the late 1990s requiring ten percent of cars sold in that state to have zero-emissions of pollutants. With approximately forty million people, the largest population in the United States, this is a substantial number of cars. This law gave a boost to the manufacturing of hydrogen fuel celled cars by the big automobile makers. Despite these successes, there is still a long road ahead for the hydrogen economy. The world's infrastructure is run on oil and oil products. Massive expenditures would be required to transform our system to a hydrogen-based one, and many underdeveloped countries are unable to afford such a transformation. **Finally, oil companies themselves are resisting the move with the specter of massive losses in revenue for decreasing oil sales staring them in the face.** One day, people may no longer need oil, but that day is long off indeed.

8. Which of the sentences below best expresses the essential information in the highlighted sentence in the passage? *Incorrect* answer choices change the meaning in important ways or leave out essential information.

   Ⓐ Oil companies are losing a lot of money by refusing to participate in the hydrogen economy.

   Ⓑ The big amounts of money that oil companies have already lost are making them resist hydrogen cars.

   Ⓒ With the possibility of losing a lot of money, oil companies are not favorable to the hydrogen economy.

   Ⓓ Since oil companies have to cope with their decreasing oil sales, they have no interest in hydrogen cars.

There has been some aid in this progress from various governments. ■ California passed a bill in the late 1990s requiring ten percent of cars sold in that state to have zero-emissions of pollutants. ■ With approximately forty million people, the largest population in the United States, this is a substantial number of cars. ■ This law gave a boost to the manufacturing of hydrogen fuel celled cars by the big automobile makers. ■ Despite these successes, there is still a long road ahead for the hydrogen economy. The world's infrastructure is run on oil and oil products. Massive expenditures would be required to transform our system to a hydrogen-based one, and many underdeveloped countries are unable to afford such a transformation. Finally, oil companies themselves are resisting the move with the specter of massive losses in revenue for decreasing oil sales staring them in the face. One day, people may no longer need oil, but that day is long off indeed.

9. Look at the four squares [■] that indicate where the following sentence could be added to the passage.

Ironically, considering the law, the governor of California used to drive around town in a gas-guzzling Humvee.

Where would the sentence best fit?

Click on a square [■] to add the sentence to the passage.

10 Directions: An introductory sentence for a brief summary of the passage is provided below. Complete the summary by selecting the THREE answer choices that express the most important ideas of the passage. Some sentences do not belong because they express ideas that are not presented in the passage or are minor ideas in the passage. **This question is worth 2 points.**

Drag your answer choices to the spaces where they belong.
To remove an answer choice, click on it. To review the passage, click on **View Text**.

Although a hydrogen economy is becoming more of a possibility, there are many obstacles to overcome before it will totally replace the petroleum-based infrastructure.

-
-
-

Answer Choices

1. Oil companies, the main opponents of hydrogen power, will not easily give up the profits they glean from petroleum.

2. People are reluctant to try new hydrogen cars because they think the cars are not practical without a supporting infrastructure.

3. Hydrogen must be separated from other sources in order to be used as a fuel source, and it is expensive to do so.

4. It is predicted that sometime in the future, our sources of oil will dry up, which will cause people to seek other forms of energy.

5. Hydrogen is a clean alternative to oil, which is one of the main causes of pollution throughout the planet.

6. The petroleum infrastructure of the world will be expensive to replace, and many countries cannot afford it at present.

The Disappearing Menhaden

A gulf menhaden

Most people have never heard of it, and they certainly have not eaten it in its original form, but menhaden is the most important fish in the ocean. However, it is disappearing at an alarming rate. The east coast of the United States once teemed with immense schools, some as many as a mile across, but the devastation of menhaden stocks over the last sixty years has led to severe dislocations in the oceans' ecosystems. The decline of the menhaden has had particularly disastrous effects on fish species that feed on it, on bird species that use it as a food source, and on how clean the oceans are.

Menhaden is a small fish belonging to the haddock family, and it is not very palatable to humans as it has a foul, oily taste and has numerous small bones. Commercial fishing of menhaden since the end of World War II has primarily been for the production of feed for livestock with ground-up fish used to make meal for chickens, pigs, and cows. Companies use spotter planes to find large schools and direct fishing boats to the locations. Catches have declined almost forty percent since the 1960s and show no sign of leveling off or increasing. Unlike other species that are protected by government quotas, menhaden is not, most likely because it is not a species consumed directly by humans. This is unfortunate since the loss of menhaden spells an eco-disaster of epic proportions.

Of principal importance are the many species of fish and other animals that feed on menhaden. It is the main fish consumed by bluefish and striped bass, and both species have shown a serious decline in numbers. The striped bass was once the prized catch of the Chesapeake Bay area, but specimens brought in by rod and reel now are much smaller compared to the past. Not only do they lack the bulk of their ancestors, but they are also dying at alarming rates. Fish are not the only predators of menhaden as birds also depend on it as a source of nourishment. Large colonies of osprey all along the eastern seaboard have disappeared in recent years with the numbers of nests and birds reduced by fifty percent in some areas over the last ten years. There are similar statistics for loons in Chesapeake Bay.

  The greatest threat from the loss of the menhaden is that the oceans have lost one of their great natural filterers. Menhaden swim in massive schools with their mouths open, allowing water to flow through their gills, which absorb oxygen and grab plankton and other detritus from the water. They act like gigantic vacuum cleaners for the ocean. The cleaner water allows sunlight to penetrate to greater depths, which stimulates plant life that harbors other fish and shellfish and produces oxygen for the water. With the decline of menhaden, this process is in serious jeopardy. Chemical run-off from farms, lawns, and houses ends up in the oceans, increasing the nitrogen and phosphorus levels in the water. **Algae** grow in great numbers in these conditions, block sunlight, and deplete the water of oxygen. Entire coastal areas are lifeless as algae kill the fish. Menhaden had reduced the levels of these elements, but now that there are fewer menhaden, algae have taken over.

  Large companies that process menhaden disagree with the findings of environmental scientists. Since there is no accurate way to count the number of menhaden in the oceans, they claim that the fewer menhaden are a result of a cyclical event and that the stocks will increase again in time. Yet much of the menhaden catch consists of smaller fish, often less than one year old. These fish have not had a chance to mature long enough to become reproductive, and thus commercial fishing companies are destroying future menhaden stocks to profit at the moment. The largest companies have had to lay off many employees, and many of their vessels sit idle at wharfs. In the long run, menhaden will probably rebound once its numbers have reached the point where catching it is no longer profitable. Hopefully, laws will soon be in place to protect it from its greatest predator, mankind.

Glossary

alga: a plant that has no roots, stems, or leaves and grows in water or in other wet places

The Disappearing Menhaden

1 → Most people have never heard of it, and they certainly have not eaten it in its original form, but menhaden is the most important fish in the ocean. However, it is disappearing at an alarming rate. The east coast of the United States once teemed with immense schools, some as many as a mile across, but the devastation of menhaden stocks over the last sixty years has led to severe dislocations in the oceans' ecosystems. The decline of the menhaden has had particularly disastrous effects on fish species that feed on it, on bird species that use it as a food source, and on how clean the oceans are.

11. According to paragraph 1, the Atlantic Ocean menhaden is

   A quite well known to most people in the United States
   B eaten in great amounts not only by other fish but also by humans
   C not in any immediate danger of disappearing from the ocean
   D eaten by birds and other fish as a part of their diets

2 → Menhaden is a small fish belonging to the haddock family, and it is not very palatable to humans as it has a foul, oily taste and has numerous small bones. Commercial fishing of menhaden since the end of World War II has primarily been for the production of feed for livestock with ground-up fish used to make meal for chickens, pigs, and cows. Companies use spotter planes to find large schools and direct fishing boats to the locations. Catches have declined almost forty percent since the 1960s and show no sign of leveling off or increasing. Unlike other species that are protected by government quotas, menhaden is not, most likely because it is not a species consumed directly by humans. This is unfortunate since the loss of menhaden spells an eco-disaster of epic proportions.

12 The word "palatable" in the passage is closest in meaning to
   Ⓐ partial
   Ⓑ edible
   Ⓒ disgusting
   Ⓓ stable

13 The word "epic" in the passage is closest in meaning to
   Ⓐ disastrous
   Ⓑ massive
   Ⓒ strange
   Ⓓ worldwide

14 In paragraph 2, the author's description of menhaden mentions all of the following EXCEPT:
   Ⓐ The lack of laws providing government protection
   Ⓑ The technology used to catch it in the oceans
   Ⓒ The desire of people to consume it as food
   Ⓓ The primary manner in which it is used

Of principal importance are the many species of fish and other animals that feed on menhaden. It is the main fish consumed by bluefish and striped bass, and both species have shown a serious decline in numbers. The striped bass was once the prized catch of the Chesapeake Bay area, but specimens brought in by rod and reel now are much smaller compared to the past. Not only do they lack the bulk of their ancestors, but they are also dying at alarming rates. Fish are not the only predators of menhaden as birds also depend on it as a source of nourishment. Large colonies of osprey all along the eastern seaboard have disappeared in recent years with the numbers of nests and birds reduced by fifty percent in some areas over the last ten years. There are similar statistics for loons in Chesapeake Bay.

15 Which of the sentences below best expresses the essential information in the highlighted sentence in the passage? *Incorrect* answer choices change the meaning in important ways or leave out essential information.

Ⓐ There are prizes given for the best striped bass caught by sport fishermen in Chesapeake Bay.

Ⓑ The striped bass caught by sport fishermen in Chesapeake Bay are not as large as those caught in the past.

Ⓒ The Chesapeake Bay area is well known for the striped bass that can be caught by fishermen there.

Ⓓ In the past, the Chesapeake Bay striped bass fishery was more valuable than it is nowadays.

⁴ ➜ The greatest threat from the loss of the menhaden is that the oceans have lost one of their great natural filterers. Menhaden swim in massive schools with their mouths open, allowing water to flow through their gills, which absorb oxygen and grab plankton and other detritus from the water. They act like gigantic vacuum cleaners for the ocean. The cleaner water allows sunlight to penetrate to greater depths, which stimulates plant life that harbors other fish and shellfish and produces oxygen for the water. With the decline of menhaden, this process is in serious jeopardy. Chemical run-off from farms, lawns, and houses ends up in the oceans, increasing the nitrogen and phosphorus levels in the water. **Algae** grow in great numbers in these conditions, block sunlight, and deplete the water of oxygen. Entire coastal areas are lifeless as algae kill the fish. Menhaden had reduced the levels of these elements, but now that there are fewer menhaden, algae have taken over.

16. According to paragraph 4, the main influence on the oceans as a result of declining menhaden numbers is

   Ⓐ an increase in the number of lifeless areas
   Ⓑ an overabundance of plankton near the coast
   Ⓒ the decline of fish stocks that feed on menhaden
   Ⓓ increased human dumping of chemicals in the ocean

Glossary
alga: a plant that has no roots, stems, or leaves and grows in water or in other wet places

⁵ ➔ Large companies that process menhaden disagree with the findings of environmental scientists. Since there is no accurate way to count the number of menhaden in the oceans, they claim that the fewer menhaden are a result of a cyclical event and that the stocks will increase again in time. Yet much of the menhaden catch consists of smaller fish, often less than one year old. These fish have not had a chance to mature long enough to become reproductive, and thus commercial fishing companies are destroying future menhaden stocks to profit at the moment. The largest companies have had to lay off many employees, and many of their vessels sit idle at wharfs. In the long run, menhaden will probably rebound once its numbers have reached the point where catching it is no longer profitable. Hopefully, laws will soon be in place to protect it from its greatest predator, mankind.

17 The author discusses "commercial fishing companies" in paragraph 5 in order to
- Ⓐ agree with their opinions on menhaden
- Ⓑ point out the harm that they are causing
- Ⓒ criticize them for making menhaden endangered
- Ⓓ suggest ways that they could protect menhaden

18 According to paragraph 5, fishing companies argue that shrinking menhaden stocks are the result of
- Ⓐ a normal cycle that will end sometime in the near future
- Ⓑ environmental factors that are totally beyond their control
- Ⓒ fishing technology that has developed in recent years
- Ⓓ a lack of oxygen in the ocean as a result of too much algae

The greatest threat from the loss of the menhaden is that the oceans have lost one of their great natural filterers. Menhaden swim in massive schools with their mouths open, allowing water to flow through their gills, which absorb oxygen and grab plankton and other detritus from the water. They act like gigantic vacuum cleaners for the ocean. The cleaner water allows sunlight to penetrate to greater depths, which stimulates plant life that harbors other fish and shellfish and produces oxygen for the water. ■ With the decline of menhaden, this process is in serious jeopardy. ■ Chemical run-off from farms, lawns, and houses ends up in the oceans, increasing the nitrogen and phosphorus levels in the water. ■ **Algae** grow in great numbers in these conditions, block sunlight, and deplete the water of oxygen. ■ Entire coastal areas are lifeless as algae kill the fish. Menhaden had reduced the levels of these elements, but now that there are fewer menhaden, algae have taken over.

19 Look at the four squares [■] that indicate where the following sentence could be added to the passage.

In addition, algae sink to the ocean floor and prevent shellfish and oxygen-producing plants from growing.

Where would the sentence best fit?

Click on a square [■] to add the sentence to the passage.

📄 *Glossary*
alga: a plant that has no roots, stems, or leaves and grows in water or in other wet places

20 Directions: An introductory sentence for a brief summary of the passage is provided below. Complete the summary by selecting the THREE answer choices that express the most important ideas of the passage. Some sentences do not belong because they express ideas that are not presented in the passage or are minor ideas in the passage. **This question is worth 2 points.**

Drag your answer choices to the spaces where they belong.
To remove an answer choice, click on it. To review the passage, click on **View Text**.

The decline of menhaden stocks in the oceans is causing a great amount of harm.

-
-
-

Answer Choices

1. Improvements in fishing methods have resulted in larger catches in the last few decades that have depleted the stocks.

2. The loss of menhaden has caused an increase in oxygen-destroying algae and created dead zones in the ocean.

3. Despite a great deal of evidence, commercial fishing companies refuse to recognize that the number of menhaden is declining.

4. Many fish and bird species are disappearing because they depend on menhaden as one of their main sources of food.

5. Unless the government passes laws to protect menhaden, it will decline until there is no more profit in fishing for it.

6. People have developed a taste for menhaden, which is one of the reasons that fishing for it has increased.

How to Master Skills for the TOEFL® iBT

Actual Test
READING 1

06

Reading Section Directions

This section measures your ability to understand academic passages in English. You will have **35 minutes** to read and answer questions about **2 passages**. A clock at the top of the screen will show you how much time is remaining.

Most questions are worth 1 point but the last question for each passage is worth more than 1 point. The directions for the last question indicate how many points you may receive.

Some passages include a word or phrase that is **underlined** in blue. Click on the word or phrase to see a definition or an explanation.

When you want to move to the next question, click on **Next**. You may skip questions and go back to them later. If you want to return to previous questions, click on **Back**. You can click on **Review** at any time, and the review screen will show you which questions you have answered and which you have not answered. From this review screen, you may go directly to any question you have already seen in the Reading section.

Click on **Continue** to go on.

Solving Stuttering

   Stuttering is the inability to form words or sentences at what is considered a normal speed of speech. Stutterers drag out every syllable and sound, for what seems to the listener to be an eternity, just to say simple things such as their name or to ask a basic question. The degree of stuttering varies, and some stutterers have very good periods when they have no difficulty **articulating** at a normal pace. Around one percent of the American population stutters to some degree with men being four times more likely than women to be stutterers. Doctors, speech therapists, and psychologists in the past puzzled over the causes of stuttering and usually determined that it is related to the way a child is brought up or some traumatic incident in childhood. The newest theories on stuttering concentrate on how the brain functions during speech and have concluded that stuttering is the result of the brain thinking too much while speaking.

   Imagine a baseball player performing a complicated action such as hitting a home run. Almost all his actions are instinctive, are based on years of practice, and happen sometimes even without knowledge of how the player performed such a feat. Imagine what would happen if he thought through each individual step before doing it. Time is against him, and he would fail. The ball would whip by, and he would strike out, standing there with the bat on his shoulder. This is what goes on in the mind of a stutterer. Each sound is thought of and analyzed before it is articulated. Speech is one of the most complicated actions humans perform with almost every facial muscle, the tongue, the vocal cords, the lungs, and the brain working in concert to create it. The brain is wired to perform these tasks in correct order in just the right amount for each part and to do so without the person being conscious of the actions happening.

   The stutterer trips over words on account of examining each part carefully before saying it, like children learning a long, complicated word they are seeing for the first time. Specialists believe that stutterers are listening to themselves as they talk but at a subconscious level of understanding. When a stutterer tries to increase the tempo of his speech, his brain cannot keep up with the pattern of recognition of what is said, and a loop occurs, causing him to repeat the same sound or word over and over again.

   Speech therapists are using a method called delayed audio feedback to help stutterers. A stutterer carries a portable device that allows him to hear his own words with a time delay, so he hears what he said a few milliseconds later. This operates on the principle of the crowded room. In a crowded room, a stutterer has very few problems making himself understood because the greater background noise does not allow him to hear his own voice as clearly. For example, a man at a party seems fine talking to people in the crowd, but if he is asked to make a speech, he will freeze up and start to stutter as everyone falls silent to listen to him. His brain now concentrates on what he is saying instead of the other people, and it has more time to think and thus slow down the man's speech patterns. The delayed audio feedback device acts as a substitute for the crowd, bringing noise to the ear as the brain is about to start thinking too much about the next word that should be said.

There are different opinions on the effectiveness of delayed audio feedback. Some experts are enthusiastic about it while others say it is only effective for a few months, after which the brain becomes familiar with the device and adjusts to it. Specialists have examined stutterers' brain functions with MRI technology and have discovered that they rely less on the left hemisphere of the brain, the side that controls speech functions. Future studies of the brain may make it possible to create microchips that can be implanted, thereby curing stutterers of their affliction for good. This may smack of science fiction, but for stutterers, it will surely be a welcome advance.

Glossary
articulate: to speak clearly

Solving Stuttering

1 → Stuttering is the inability to form words or sentences at what is considered a normal speed of speech. Stutterers drag out every syllable and sound, for what seems to the listener to be an eternity, just to say simple things such as their name or to ask a basic question. The degree of stuttering varies, and some stutterers have very good periods when they have no difficulty **articulating** at a normal pace. Around one percent of the American population stutters to some degree with men being four times more likely than women to be stutterers. Doctors, speech therapists, and psychologists in the past puzzled over the causes of stuttering and usually determined that it is related to the way a child is brought up or some traumatic incident in childhood. The newest theories on stuttering concentrate on how the brain functions during speech and have concluded that stuttering is the result of the brain thinking too much while speaking.

Glossary
articulate: to speak clearly

1. According to paragraph 1, stutterer's main speech problem is
   - (A) their pronunciation of words
   - (B) the rate at which they speak
   - (C) their inability to recall words
   - (D) being unable to ask simple questions

2. In paragraph 1, the author's description of reasons for stuttering mentions all of the following EXCEPT:
   - (A) Parental rearing methods
   - (B) The gender which one is
   - (C) A terrible incident as a child
   - (D) A problem with brain functions

2 → Imagine a baseball player performing a complicated action such as hitting a home run. Almost all his actions are instinctive, are based on years of practice, and happen sometimes even without knowledge of how the player performed such a feat. Imagine what would happen if he thought through each individual step before doing it. Time is against him, and he would fail. The ball would whip by, and he would strike out, standing there with the bat on his shoulder. This is what goes on in the mind of a stutterer. Each sound is thought of and analyzed before it is articulated. Speech is one of the most complicated actions humans perform with almost every facial muscle, the tongue, the vocal cords, the lungs, and the brain working in concert to create it. The brain is wired to perform these tasks in correct order in just the right amount for each part and to do so without the person being conscious of the actions happening.

3. Which of the sentences below best expresses the essential information in the highlighted sentence in the passage? *Incorrect* answer choices change the meaning in important ways or leave out essential information.

   A. The player would not know how to perform the action without years of practice and his instincts.
   B. Instinctively, the player is aware that only practice has allowed him to perform this complicated action.
   C. The player's instincts allow him to perform great actions even when he is unaware of what he is doing.
   D. Years of practice allow the player instinctively to perform an action without knowing how he did it.

4. According to paragraph 2, speech is complicated because

   A. the brain needs to work very fast to get all the words out
   B. every facial muscle must be used to make sounds
   C. multiple body parts are involved in creating human speech
   D. speed is essential in all aspects of making voiced sounds

The stutterer trips over words on account of examining each part carefully before saying it, like children learning a long, complicated word they are seeing for the first time. Specialists believe that stutterers are listening to themselves as they talk but at a **subconscious** level of understanding. When a stutterer tries to increase the tempo of his speech, his brain cannot keep up with the pattern of recognition of what is said, and a loop occurs, causing him to repeat the same sound or word over and over again.

5. The word "**subconscious**" in the passage is closest in meaning to
   - (A) unknown
   - (B) hidden
   - (C) false
   - (D) forbidden

⁴ ➜ Speech therapists are using a method called delayed audio feedback to help stutterers. A stutterer carries a portable device that allows him to hear his own words with a time delay, so he hears what he said a few milliseconds later. This operates on the principle of the crowded room. In a crowded room, a stutterer has very few problems making himself understood because the greater background noise does not allow him to hear his own voice as clearly. For example, a man at a party seems fine talking to people in the crowd, but if he is asked to make a speech, he will freeze up and start to stutter as everyone falls silent to listen to him. His brain now concentrates on what he is saying instead of the other people, and it has more time to think and thus slow down the man's speech patterns. The delayed audio feedback device acts as a substitute for the crowd, bringing noise to the ear as the brain is about to start thinking too much about the next word that should be said.

6. In paragraph 4, why does the author mention "a man at a party"?
   A To discuss how stutterers function in various social situations
   B To examine the reactions of a stutterer asked to make a speech
   C To explore how the delayed audio feedback theory was developed
   D To explain the theory as to why delayed audio feedback works

7. According to paragraph 4, delayed audio feedback helps a stutterer by
   A allowing him to think clearly before speaking by looping his speech
   B distracting his brain so he does not think too much about his next words
   C making him able to speak clearly in social situations such as parties
   D confusing him into thinking that he is speaking in a crowded room

5 → There are different opinions on the effectiveness of delayed audio feedback. Some experts are enthusiastic about it while others say it is only effective for a few months, after which the brain becomes familiar with the device and adjusts to it. Specialists have examined stutterers' brain functions with MRI technology and have discovered that they rely less on the left hemisphere of the brain, the side that controls speech functions. Future studies of the brain may make it possible to create microchips that can be implanted, thereby curing stutterers of their affliction for good. This may smack of science fiction, but for stutterers, it will surely be a welcome advance.

8. It can be inferred from paragraph 5 that microchips for the brain

   Ⓐ have already been implanted in the brains of some stutterers
   Ⓑ have already been developed for stutterers to make use of
   Ⓒ have not been implanted in stutterers but have been created
   Ⓓ have neither been created nor implanted in any stutterers

Stuttering is the inability to form words or sentences at what is considered a normal speed of speech. Stutterers drag out every syllable and sound, for what seems to the listener to be an eternity, just to say simple things such as their name or to ask a basic question. The degree of stuttering varies, and some stutterers have very good periods when they have no difficulty **articulating** at a normal pace. ■ Around one percent of the American population stutters to some degree with men being four times more likely than women to be stutterers. ■ Doctors, speech therapists, and psychologists in the past puzzled over the causes of stuttering and usually determined that it is related to the way a child is brought up or some traumatic incident in childhood. ■ The newest theories on stuttering concentrate on how the brain functions during speech and have concluded that stuttering is the result of the brain thinking too much while speaking. ■

9. Look at the four squares [■] that indicate where the following sentence could be added to the passage.

For example, in the public school system of the past, left-handed children were sometimes forced to write with their right hands, which resulted in stuttering in some.

Where would the sentence best fit?

Click on a square [■] to add the sentence to the passage.

Glossary
articulate: to speak clearly

10 Directions: An introductory sentence for a brief summary of the passage is provided below. Complete the summary by selecting the THREE answer choices that express the most important ideas of the passage. Some sentences do not belong because they express ideas that are not presented in the passage or are minor ideas in the passage. **This question is worth 2 points.**

Drag your answer choices to the spaces where they belong.
To remove an answer choice, click on it. To review the passage, click on **View Text**.

Past theories on the causes of stuttering have been replaced by a new theory.

-
-
-

Answer Choices

1. The brain is instinctual and not designed to think about problems in too much detail.

2. Images of MRI scanners show that stutterers use the part of the brain concerned with speech less than those who do not stutter.

3. Mechanical audio devices have been developed to help alleviate stuttering, but they are not supported by a majority of experts.

4. A stutterer in a crowded noisy room has a more difficult time making himself understood than if he were the only one speaking.

5. The success of delayed audio feedback devices seems to indicate that stuttering is connected to how the brain processes sound.

6. Instead of instinctually letting the brain make speech, a stutterer seems to be consciously thinking of each step.

Hispaniola Forestry Management

A map of Haiti and the Dominican Republic

An aerial view of the border between Haiti and the Dominican Republic on the Caribbean island of Hispaniola shows a remarkable sight: large pristine forests on the Dominican side and a virtually barren land on the Haitian side, a land devoid of trees except for a few small clumps. This is partially the result of nature as less frequent rains and poorer soil in Haiti mean fewer, smaller trees with very slow regrowth compared to the Dominican side. However, it is people more than nature that have determined the island's differences in forest growth. In the centuries since Europeans first colonized the island, the two nations have followed different paths of forest management, which has resulted in the current **discrepancy**. This is the result of both the history of the two nations and the policies of the people and their present-day governments.

Christopher Columbus first sighted Hispaniola in 1492, and the Spanish soon colonized it. The half-million population of Arawak Indians died of disease by 1520, and the Spaniards then imported African slaves. The Spanish kept mostly to the eastern two-thirds of the island, and a small French trading post on the western side grew into a large French colony in the remaining third. The French decided to import massive numbers of slaves to clear vast forests and to plant sugarcane, a cash crop. By the beginning of the nineteenth century, Hispaniola featured a small elite of Europeans supported by almost one million slaves, the majority on the French side.

In 1803, the western slaves rebelled and defeated a French expedition to recapture the colony. The newly independent slaves renamed their nation Haiti, divided the land amongst the people, and forbade foreigners from owning land or businesses. This legacy has had a profound impact on Haiti's development and has resulted in Haiti being the poorest nation in the Western Hemisphere. With little outside investment, the nation's elite depend on exploiting the work of **peasants**. Haiti also has the highest population density in the West with ten million people crowded into one-third of the island. Slavery's legacy led to a policy of free men owning their own land with them clearing the land for farming by cutting down trees in every direction. The nation is too poor to develop a dependable electrical or gas infrastructure, so Haitians primarily depend on charcoal for cooking fuel and burn trees to make it. Even the few protected parks in Haiti are raided for their prized trees. This has resulted in only one percent of the land remaining forested.

The Dominican Republic, while not a wealthy nation by global standards, stands head and shoulders above Haiti. The Dominicans have no history of slave rebellion, and the Spanish encouraged foreign settlement and investment on their side of the island. The Dominican Republic has more rainfall and richer soil than Haiti, which has enabled the Dominicans to produce cash export crops such as cacao, coffee, tobacco, and avocadoes. With the wealth acquired from these crops, the nation could import large numbers of gas ranges and propane tanks, which were sold to the population at discounts to encourage them not to use wood or charcoal for cooking. Politically, the Dominicans have had a series of governments concerned about the environmental protection of the nation's forests. Joaquin Balaguer, president for much of the late twentieth century, threw his energy into preserving the Dominican Republic's forests, which included making illegal logging a crime against the security of the nation. The military was charged with defending the nation's forests and received orders to kill illegal loggers who did not surrender.

The legacy of Balaguer continues to the present with the Dominican Republic having some of the Western Hemisphere's most comprehensive environmental protection laws, most of which are actually enforced. Over thirty-five percent of Dominican land is forest, most of which is protected. This is in sharp contrast to Haiti, where one can look for miles and not see a single tree. The already thin soil of Haiti is eroding and blowing away year after year, making farmers' small plots less productive. With its massive population and bleak future, many Haitians are sneaking across the border in the hope of better lives in the Dominican Republic.

Glossary
discrepancy: a difference
peasant: a farm worker, usually one who is poor

Hispaniola Forestry Management

1 → An aerial view of the border between Haiti and the Dominican Republic on the Caribbean island of Hispaniola shows a remarkable sight: large pristine forests on the Dominican side and a virtually barren land on the Haitian side, a land devoid of trees except for a few small clumps. This is partially the result of nature as less frequent rains and poorer soil in Haiti mean fewer, smaller trees with very slow regrowth compared to the Dominican side. However, it is people more than nature that have determined the island's differences in forest growth. In the centuries since Europeans first colonized the island, the two nations have followed different paths of forest management, which has resulted in the current **discrepancy**. This is the result of both the history of the two nations and the policies of the people and their present-day governments.

11 In paragraph 1, the author's description of Haiti and the Dominican Republic mentions all of the following EXCEPT:

Ⓐ The legacy of each country's history
Ⓑ The types of trees in their forests
Ⓒ The attitude of each country's government
Ⓓ The forces of nature affecting the island

📖 ***Glossary***
discrepancy: a difference

² → Christopher Columbus first sighted Hispaniola in 1492, and the Spanish soon colonized it. The half-million population of Arawak Indians died of disease by 1520, and the Spaniards then imported African slaves. The Spanish kept mostly to the eastern two-thirds of the island, and a small French trading post on the western side grew into a large French colony in the remaining third. The French decided to import massive numbers of slaves to clear vast forests and to plant sugarcane, a cash crop. By the beginning of the nineteenth century, Hispaniola featured a small elite of Europeans supported by almost one million slaves, the majority on the French side.

12 In paragraph 2, the author mentions "sugarcane" in order to

Ⓐ explain why such large parts of the forests were cut down

Ⓑ discuss the basis of the economy in that particular colony

Ⓒ show the differences between the French and Spanish colonies

Ⓓ explain why there were so many slaves working in the colony

13 It can be inferred from paragraph 2 that the Arawak Indians

Ⓐ did not live on Hispaniola together with African slaves

Ⓑ were deliberately killed by the Spanish to make room for colonists

Ⓒ went to war with the Spanish until they were finally eliminated

Ⓓ were friends with the Spanish but died in spite of this amity

³ ➡ In 1803, the western slaves rebelled and defeated a French expedition to recapture the colony. The newly independent slaves renamed their nation Haiti, divided the land amongst the people, and forbade foreigners from owning land or businesses. This legacy has had a profound impact on Haiti's development and has resulted in Haiti being the poorest nation in the Western Hemisphere. With little outside investment, the nation's elite depend on exploiting the work of **peasants**. Haiti also has the highest population density in the West with ten million people crowded into one-third of the island. Slavery's legacy led to a policy of free men owning their own land with them clearing the land for farming by cutting down trees in every direction. The nation is too poor to develop a dependable electrical or gas infrastructure, so Haitians primarily depend on charcoal for cooking fuel and burn trees to make it. Even the few protected parks in Haiti are raided for their prized trees. This has resulted in only one percent of the land remaining forested.

14 The word "profound" in the passage is closest in meaning to
  (A) powerful
  (B) potential
  (C) wide
  (D) immediate

15 According to paragraph 3, what happened after the slave rebellion in the French colony?
  (A) The French gave up the colony and left without a fight.
  (B) The French agreed to set the slaves free and departed.
  (C) The French tried to retake it but failed in their attempt.
  (D) The French succeeded in retaking it from the former slaves.

Glossary
peasant: a farm worker, usually one who is poor

4 → The Dominican Republic, while not a wealthy nation by global standards, stands head and shoulders above Haiti. The Dominicans have no history of slave rebellion, and the Spanish encouraged foreign settlement and investment on their side of the island. The Dominican Republic has more rainfall and richer soil than Haiti, which has enabled the Dominicans to produce cash export crops such as cacao, coffee, tobacco, and avocadoes. With the wealth acquired from these crops, the nation could import large numbers of gas ranges and propane tanks, which were sold to the population at discounts to encourage them not to use wood or charcoal for cooking. Politically, the Dominicans have had a series of governments concerned about the environmental protection of the nation's forests. Joaquin Balaguer, president for much of the late twentieth century, threw his energy into preserving the Dominican Republic's forests, which included making illegal logging a crime against the security of the nation. The military was charged with defending the nation's forests and received orders to kill illegal loggers who did not surrender.

16 According to paragraph 4, the Dominican Republic's military

Ⓐ cannot be corrupted by people who are interested in participating in illegal logging

Ⓑ does much of the work regarding the enforcement of the forest protection policy

Ⓒ will always shoot illegal loggers as soon as they are spotted chopping down trees

Ⓓ was ordered by Joaquin Balaguer to make protecting forests of the utmost importance

⁵ ➜ The legacy of Balaguer continues to the present with the Dominican Republic having some of the Western Hemisphere's most comprehensive environmental protection laws, most of which are actually enforced. Over thirty-five percent of Dominican land is forest, most of which is protected. This is in sharp contrast to Haiti, where one can look for miles and not see a single tree. The already thin soil of Haiti is eroding and blowing away year after year, making farmers' small plots less productive. With its massive population and bleak future, many Haitians are sneaking across the border in the hope of better lives in the Dominican Republic.

17 Which of the sentences below best expresses the essential information in the highlighted sentence in the passage? *Incorrect* answer choices change the meaning in important ways or leave out essential information.

- (A) The Dominican Republic continues to enforce Balaguer's environmental policies, making them the most thorough in the Western Hemisphere.
- (B) Balaguer's environmental policies are among the best in the Western Hemisphere, which means that they are often enforced.
- (C) Countries in the Western Hemisphere have a poor record of environmental protection and enforcement except for the Dominican Republic.
- (D) Protecting the environment was the main legacy that Balaguer left the people of the Dominican Republic when he resigned.

18 According to paragraph 5, Haitian farms are less productive because

- (A) the population of the country is too big for farmers to support
- (B) farmers are fleeing the country to work elsewhere
- (C) the topsoil on the farmland is continually disappearing
- (D) farms in the country are too small to be efficient

The Dominican Republic, while not a wealthy nation by global standards, stands head and shoulders above Haiti. The Dominicans have no history of slave rebellion, and the Spanish encouraged foreign settlement and investment on their side of the island. The Dominican Republic has more rainfall and richer soil than Haiti, which has enabled the Dominicans to produce cash export crops such as cacao, coffee, tobacco, and avocadoes. ■ With the wealth acquired from these crops, the nation could import large numbers of gas ranges and propane tanks, which were sold to the population at discounts to encourage them not to use wood or charcoal for cooking. ■ Politically, the Dominicans have had a series of governments concerned about the environmental protection of the nation's forests. ■ Joaquin Balaguer, president for much of the late twentieth century, threw his energy into preserving the Dominican Republic's forests, which included making illegal logging a crime against the security of the nation. ■ The military was charged with defending the nation's forests and received orders to kill illegal loggers who did not surrender.

19 Look at the four squares [■] that indicate where the following sentence could be added to the passage.

These governments even included that of the dictator Trujillo, who, however, was mostly interested in using forests for private profit.

Where would the sentence best fit?

Click on a square [■] to add the sentence to the passage.

20 Directions: An introductory sentence for a brief summary of the passage is provided below. Complete the summary by selecting the THREE answer choices that express the most important ideas of the passage. Some sentences do not belong because they express ideas that are not presented in the passage or are minor ideas in the passage. **This question is worth 2 points.**

Drag your answer choices to the spaces where they belong.
To remove an answer choice, click on it. To review the passage, click on **View Text**.

Haiti and the Dominican Republic are located on the same island but have vastly different forest management policies.

-
-
-

Answer Choices

1. The Dominican Republic's government is concerned about the environment and carefully manages forests.

2. Haiti is much poorer than the Dominican Republic, and it also has many fewer trees.

3. Haitians often cut down trees to make charcoal in order to use it as cooking fuel.

4. Haiti was founded when slaves on the island revolted and killed all of the French there.

5. The lack of trees in Haiti is causing the land to be eroded, which makes farming difficult.

6. Satellite pictures of the Dominican Republic and Haiti show that the two countries look very different.

How to Master Skills for the TOEFL® iBT

Actual Test
READING 1

07

TOEFL READING

Reading Section Directions

This section measures your ability to understand academic passages in English. You will have **35 minutes** to read and answer questions about **2 passages**. A clock at the top of the screen will show you how much time is remaining.

Most questions are worth 1 point but the last question for each passage is worth more than 1 point. The directions for the last question indicate how many points you may receive.

Some passages include a word or phrase that is **underlined** in blue. Click on the word or phrase to see a definition or an explanation.

When you want to move to the next question, click on **Next**. You may skip questions and go back to them later. If you want to return to previous questions, click on **Back**. You can click on **Review** at any time, and the review screen will show you which questions you have answered and which you have not answered. From this review screen, you may go directly to any question you have already seen in the Reading section.

Click on **Continue** to go on.

How Plants Recognize Seasons

As a general rule, plants such as trees and flowers begin growing leaves and flowers in spring and develop fully by summer. Some may bear fruit in the summer season whereas others do so during autumn. In autumn, the leaves of trees change colors and fall off while flowers stop blooming and begin to wither. In winter, flowers die while trees are stripped of their leaves and enter a period of dormancy until spring returns. Something that many botanists have wondered is how plants recognize the seasons and when they need to undergo various changes. Many believe they may know the answer to this question.

The Earth is tilted on its axis, resulting in either the northern or southern half of the planet receiving more direct sunlight from the sun than the other half. As the Earth orbits the sun, which half of the Earth is tilting away from the sun changes and causes the changing of the seasons. For instance, when the North Pole is tilted in the direction of the sun, the Northern Hemisphere experiences summer. When the South Pole is tilted toward the sun, the Northern Hemisphere is experiencing winter. As the seasons change, so does the amount of sunlight that reaches the planet's surface in different places. This, in turn, affects both local temperatures as well as the length of the day, which determines how much sunlight an area receives.

Over time, plants have evolved to develop **photoreceptors** to detect various changes in temperature and sunlight, and they cause plants to behave differently each season. The photoreceptors allow plants to identify the intensity and duration of sunlight as well as its quality— that is, determining how much warmth the sunlight provides. The photoreceptors also inform plants what the season is and from which direction the light is coming, which permits plants to adapt to their current environment and to grow as well as possible. For instance, photoreceptors can trigger the activation of various hormones in plants which determine whether they should bloom or release their leaves depending upon how much light has been measured.

How photoreceptors influence plants can be clearly seen in how many plants grow throughout the year. In spring, each day is no longer as short as it was in winter, and temperatures tend to increase, which photoreceptors pick up on, so plants start growing. Summer features long days full of sunlight and warm temperatures, which are ideal conditions for photosynthesis. Plants become larger, blossom and bloom, and grow fruit during this season. When fall arrives, the days start becoming shorter and shorter while temperatures decline, so plants release their leaves, slow down their **metabolism**, and store energy to help them survive winter. During winter, the days are the shortest of the year, and there is little sunlight or warmth, so plants stay dormant until spring once again returns.

Another factor that some plants use to determine what to do is the temperature. When winter begins to come to an end and spring approaches, the weather starts becoming warmer. Some plants, such as peach trees, are capable of measuring the temperature. They can tell how warm or cold the air is and for how long it remains at a certain temperature. When there are only a certain number of cold hours in a day, an internal signal may be sent to peach trees that enables them to blossom. Azaleas, a type of flowering shrub known for their beautiful flowers, behave in a similar manner.

Yet another way that some plants determine the changing of the seasons is by monitoring the amount of darkness each day. This is crucial to certain plants because, depending on the amount of darkness, various hormones and proteins that assist with their growth can be produced by them. Flowering plants can be divided into two categories: short-day plants and long-day plants. Short-day plants, which include chrysanthemums, poinsettias, violets, rice, and soybeans, flower when days are shorter. On the other hand, long-day plants flower when days are longer and include plants such as lettuce, spinach, potatoes, asters, and hibiscus. The life cycles of these plants are therefore determined by light or darkness, so they behave differently as the seasons change.

Glossary
photoreceptor: a group of cells that are stimulated by light
metabolism: a group of chemical reactions in organisms that keep them alive

How Plants Recognize Seasons

1 → As a general rule, plants such as trees and flowers begin growing leaves and flowers in spring and develop fully by summer. Some may bear fruit in the summer season whereas others do so during autumn. In autumn, the leaves of trees change colors and fall off while flowers stop blooming and begin to wither. In winter, flowers die while trees are stripped of their leaves and enter a period of dormancy until spring returns. Something that many botanists have wondered is how plants recognize the seasons and when they need to undergo various changes. Many believe they may know the answer to this question.

1. Which of the following can be inferred from paragraph 1 about plants?
   - Ⓐ All plants lose their leaves during either fall or winter.
   - Ⓑ They are capable of growing fruit in three of the four seasons.
   - Ⓒ Scientists are positive they know why plants change each season.
   - Ⓓ Not all of them develop flowers during spring or summer.

2 → The Earth is tilted on its axis, resulting in either the northern or southern half of the planet receiving more direct sunlight from the sun than the other half. As the Earth orbits the sun, which half of the Earth is tilting away from the sun changes and causes the changing of the seasons. For instance, when the North Pole is tilted in the direction of the sun, the Northern Hemisphere experiences summer. When the South Pole is tilted toward the sun, the Northern Hemisphere is experiencing winter. As the seasons change, so does the amount of sunlight that reaches the planet's surface in different places. This, in turn, affects both local temperatures as well as the length of the day, which determines how much sunlight an area receives.

2. In paragraph 2, the author's description of the seasons mentions which of the following?
   A How long each season lasts
   B What causes them to change
   C When each part of the Earth has winter
   D How temperatures affect them

3. In paragraph 2, all of the following questions are answered EXCEPT:
   A What are factors that contribute to areas of the Earth getting sunlight?
   B What is the North Pole like when the Northern Hemisphere has winter?
   C Why does half of the Earth receive more sunlight than the other half?
   D Which season sees the ground receiving the largest amount of sunlight?

Over time, plants have evolved to develop **photoreceptors** to detect various changes in temperature and sunlight, and they cause plants to behave differently each season. The photoreceptors allow plants to identify the intensity and duration of sunlight as well as its quality—that is, determining how much warmth the sunlight provides. The photoreceptors also inform plants what the season is and from which direction the light is coming, which permits plants to adapt to their current environment and to grow as well as possible. For instance, photoreceptors can trigger the activation of various hormones in plants which determine whether they should bloom or release their leaves depending upon how much light has been measured.

4. The word "they" in the passage refers to
   A) plants
   B) photoreceptors
   C) various changes
   D) temperature and sunlight

5. Which of the sentences below best expresses the essential information in the highlighted sentence in the passage? *Incorrect* answer choices change the meaning in important ways or leave out essential information.
   A) Plants are able to know when to do activities such as blooming and shedding leaves based upon hormones that are released by them.
   B) Hormones are responsible for photoreceptors in plants that help them do various actions which are determined by the changing of seasons.
   C) When hormones in plants measure certain amounts of light, their photoreceptors tell them whether to blossom or to make their leaves fall off.
   D) Photoreceptors are responsible for activating hormones that tell plants to bloom or lose leaves based on the amount of light they are getting.

📖 *Glossary*

photoreceptor: a group of cells that are stimulated by light

How photoreceptors influence plants can be clearly seen in how many plants grow throughout the year. In spring, each day is no longer as short as it was in winter, and temperatures tend to increase, which photoreceptors pick up on, so plants start growing. Summer features long days full of sunlight and warm temperatures, which are ideal conditions for photosynthesis. Plants become larger, blossom and bloom, and grow fruit during this season. When fall arrives, the days start becoming shorter and shorter while temperatures decline, so plants release their leaves, slow down their **metabolism**, and store energy to help them survive winter. During winter, the days are the shortest of the year, and there is little sunlight or warmth, so plants stay dormant until spring once again returns.

6. The word "dormant" is closest in meaning to
   A) unhealthy
   B) fruitful
   C) alive
   D) inactive

📗 Glossary

metabolism: a group of chemical reactions in organisms that keep them alive

5 → Another factor that some plants use to determine what to do is the temperature. When winter begins to come to an end and spring approaches, the weather starts becoming warmer. Some plants, such as peach trees, are capable of measuring the temperature. They can tell how warm or cold the air is and for how long it remains at a certain temperature. When there are only a certain number of cold hours in a day, an internal signal may be sent to peach trees that enables them to blossom. Azaleas, a type of flowering shrub known for their beautiful flowers, behave in a similar manner.

6 → Yet another way that some plants determine the changing of the seasons is by monitoring the amount of darkness each day. This is crucial to certain plants because, depending on the amount of darkness, various hormones and proteins that assist with their growth can be produced by them. Flowering plants can be divided into two categories: short-day plants and long-day plants. Short-day plants, which include chrysanthemums, poinsettias, violets, rice, and soybeans, flower when days are shorter. On the other hand, long-day plants flower when days are longer and include plants such as lettuce, spinach, potatoes, asters, and hibiscus. The life cycles of these plants are therefore determined by light or darkness, so they behave differently as the seasons change.

7. In paragraph 5, the author uses "peach trees" as an example of
   Ⓐ trees that are similar to azaleas in the beauty of their flowers
   Ⓑ plants that blossom based upon how cold the weather is
   Ⓒ trees that are capable of blossoming even in cool weather
   Ⓓ plants that measure temperature to determine when their leaves grow

8. According to paragraph 6, which of the following is true of rice and soybeans?
   Ⓐ They are in the same family of plants as violets and poinsettias.
   Ⓑ They are important grains that people around the world consume.
   Ⓒ They undergo life cycles similar to those of spinach and potatoes.
   Ⓓ They produce blossoms during times with few daylight hours.

How photoreceptors influence plants can be clearly seen in how many plants grow throughout the year. In spring, each day is no longer as short as it was in winter, and temperatures tend to increase, which photoreceptors pick up on, so plants start growing. ■ Summer features long days full of sunlight and warm temperatures, which are ideal conditions for photosynthesis. ■ Plants become larger, blossom and bloom, and grow fruit during this season. ■ When fall arrives, the days start becoming shorter and shorter while temperatures decline, so plants release their leaves, slow down their **metabolism**, and store energy to help them survive winter. ■ During winter, the days are the shortest of the year, and there is little sunlight or warmth, so plants stay dormant until spring once again returns.

Glossary

metabolism: a group of chemical reactions in organisms that keep them alive

9. Look at the four squares [■] that indicate where the following sentence could be added to the passage.

   This process provides plants with both food and energy, without which they would be unable to survive.

   Where would the sentence best fit?

   Click on a square [■] to add the sentence to the passage.

10 Directions: An introductory sentence for a brief summary of the passage is provided below. Complete the summary by selecting the THREE answer choices that express the most important ideas of the passage. Some sentences do not belong because they express ideas that are not presented in the passage or are minor ideas in the passage. **This question is worth 2 points.**

Drag your answer choices to the spaces where they belong.
To remove an answer choice, click on it. To review the passage, click on **View Text**.

Plants have various ways of detecting when the seasons change.

-
-
-

Answer Choices

1. There are short-day plants such as violets, rice, and lettuce.
2. Photoreceptors found in plants can help them tell how much sunlight there is.
3. The fact that the Earth tilts on its axis causes the seasons to change.
4. The Northern and Southern hemispheres experience different seasons.
5. The amount of sunlight and darkness indicates when some plants blossom.
6. Plants such as azaleas and peach trees can determine the air temperature.

The Global Positioning System

A GPS navigation system in a car

Getting from place to place has been a challenge for humans since the beginning of man's existence. Not only do people struggle with the actual physical problems of travel, but they also need to know the right direction to go. In one's own little part of the world, this may have been relatively easy, but as humans began traveling more, it became necessary to determine how to get from one place to another and back again. Paths, roads, and trails made journeys easier, and the creation of maps transmitted this knowledge to others.

However, once humans pushed onto the vast oceans, there were no roads or accurate maps. The compass, showing magnetic north, was a great, yet imperfect, aid. Latitude could be measured by sun angles, but until the perfection of timepieces in the nineteenth century, it was almost impossible to measure longitude. Fortunately, today there is a device which allows people easily to find their position no matter where they are: the Global Positioning System (GPS).

The Global Positioning System consists of a series of twenty-four satellites in geosynchronous orbit around Earth at an altitude of 12,500 miles. These satellites are in fixed positions, so by reading a signal from three of them, a person holding a GPS receiver can know his precise location. The GPS receiver synchronizes its clock with that of the satellites' atomic clocks. The receiver then measures how long it takes a signal from one satellite to reach it and calculates the distance from the satellite. At the same time, it is calculating the distance from two other satellites in a process called **triangulation**. Once these calculations take place, the receiver knows exactly where a person is and shows the coordinates. On more modern devices used in vehicles, it even shows an animated car right where it is on a city grid.

This miraculous system is the legacy of the United States military. When the Russians launched the world's first satellite, *Sputnik*, in 1957, many scientists immediately grasped that satellites could be used for navigation purposes. By 1964, four American satellites were being used to help American naval vessels navigate. Called Transit, the system took up to ninety minutes to give a position report, which was too slow for ever-changing battlefield situations. With the advent of the Vietnam War, the Air Force and the Army wanted a system to help them navigate the jungles of Southeast Asia. Unfortunately, the Navy, the Air Force, and the Army competed to build different systems, wasting resources and time by creating three systems instead of one.

This changed in August 1973. The Department of Defense ordered Air Force Colonel Brad Parkinson to head a team to create a navigation system that all three branches of the military and civilians could utilize. If anyone can be called the father of GPS, Parkinson deserves the title. Putting aside service rivalries, Parkinson's team created a plan implementing aspects of all three services' systems. By 1978, the system was ready and being tested, and the eventual cost of the system was four billion dollars. The military, afraid that rival countries and civilians would use the system to attack the United States or for criminal purposes, installed a distortion in the GPS signal that led to a slight error in civilian GPS receivers. Military units had a way to eliminate the error. In 2000, the American president had the distortion eliminated.

The applications of GPS are wide ranging. Police, fire, and other emergency services around the world have made it part of their standard operating equipment. It is even used to track prisoners on day leave or parole. By the turn of the century, GPS receiving devices became more inexpensive and are now affordable for much of the public. They are standard in most new car designs and are a favorite of hunters and fishermen making long treks in the wilderness. In addition, parents can fit their children with miniature tracking devices so that they can use GPS to know where their children are at all times. While many anxious parents welcome this aspect of technology, others are already beginning to wonder if the GPS revolution is just another way for the government to infringe on its citizens' privacy.

Glossary
triangulation: a method for measuring distances

The Global Positioning System

Getting from place to place has been a challenge for humans since the beginning of man's existence. Not only do people struggle with the actual physical problems of travel, but they also need to know the right direction to go. In one's own little part of the world, this may have been relatively easy, but as humans began traveling more, it became necessary to determine how to get from one place to another and back again. Paths, roads, and trails made journeys easier, and the creation of maps transmitted this knowledge to others.

2 → However, once humans pushed onto the vast oceans, there were no roads or accurate maps. The compass, showing magnetic north, was a great, yet imperfect, aid. Latitude could be measured by sun angles, but until the perfection of timepieces in the nineteenth century, it was almost impossible to measure longitude. Fortunately, today there is a device which allows people easily to find their position no matter where they are: the Global Positioning System (GPS).

11 The word "transmitted" in the passage is closest in meaning to
- A) passed on
- B) sent out
- C) took in
- D) moved on

12 In paragraph 2, the author's description of things used for navigation mentions all of the following EXCEPT:
- A) Maps
- B) Compasses
- C) Telescopes
- D) Sun angles

³➡ The Global Positioning System consists of a series of twenty-four satellites in geosynchronous orbit around Earth at an altitude of 12,500 miles. These satellites are in fixed positions, so by reading a signal from three of them, a person holding a GPS receiver can know his precise location. The GPS receiver synchronizes its clock with that of the satellites' atomic clocks. The receiver then measures how long it takes a signal from one satellite to reach it and calculates the distance from the satellite. At the same time, it is calculating the distance from two other satellites in a process called **triangulation**. Once these calculations take place, the receiver knows exactly where a person is and shows the coordinates. On more modern devices used in vehicles, it even shows an animated car right where it is on a city grid.

13 It can be inferred from paragraph 3 that

Ⓐ none of the twenty-four satellites has ever failed to function

Ⓑ a GPS receiver will always be in range of at least three satellites

Ⓒ GPS receivers have atomic clocks to keep track of time

Ⓓ all GPS receivers use animation that makes them user friendly

📖 Glossary
triangulation: a method for measuring distances

4 → This miraculous system is the legacy of the United States military. When the Russians launched the world's first satellite, *Sputnik*, in 1957, many scientists immediately grasped that satellites could be used for navigation purposes. By 1964, four American satellites were being used to help American naval vessels navigate. Called Transit, the system took up to ninety minutes to give a position report, which was too slow for ever-changing battlefield situations. With the advent of the Vietnam War, the Air Force and the Army wanted a system to help them navigate the jungles of Southeast Asia. Unfortunately, the Navy, the Air Force, and the Army competed to build different systems, wasting resources and time by creating three systems instead of one.

14. Which of the sentences below best expresses the essential information in the highlighted sentence in the passage? *Incorrect* answer choices change the meaning in important ways or leave out essential information.

   Ⓐ The first Russian satellite, *Sputnik*, was used for navigation by many scientists.
   Ⓑ After the launch of the Russian satellite *Sputnik*, other satellites have been used for navigation.
   Ⓒ The first satellite launch by Russians led scientists to understand that satellites could be navigation aids.
   Ⓓ Construction of the world's first satellite was crucial to being able to use other satellites for navigation.

15. According to paragraph 4, which of the following is true of the Global Positioning System?

   Ⓐ Work on it began as soon as the Soviets launched *Sputnik*.
   Ⓑ It was developed out of necessity during the Vietnam War.
   Ⓒ Its basis was the system used by the U.S. Navy called Transit.
   Ⓓ It was created during a joint operation of the U.S. military.

16. According to the paragraph 4, the biggest obstacle to creating GPS was

   Ⓐ interservice rivalries that existed in the American military
   Ⓑ not enough money being spent on research and development
   Ⓒ technological problems that prohibited building an accurate system
   Ⓓ a lack of support from the government in eliminating problems

⁵ ➜ This changed in August 1973. The Department of Defense ordered Air Force Colonel Brad Parkinson to head a team to create a navigation system that all three branches of the military and civilians could utilize. If anyone can be called the father of GPS, Parkinson deserves the title. Putting aside service rivalries, Parkinson's team created a plan implementing aspects of all three services' systems. By 1978, the system was ready and being tested, and the eventual cost of the system was four billion dollars. The military, afraid that rival countries and civilians would use the system to attack the United States or for criminal purposes, installed a distortion in the GPS signal that led to a slight error in civilian GPS receivers. Military units had a way to eliminate the error. In 2000, the American president had the distortion eliminated.

17 According to paragraph 5, the American military distorted the GPS signal because

- Ⓐ they refused to give away the secret of GPS to other countries
- Ⓑ they were concerned that the device would be used against them
- Ⓒ they wanted to prevent criminals from accessing the system
- Ⓓ it was classified technology that foreign nationals should not have

6 → The applications of GPS are wide ranging. Police, fire, and other emergency services around the world have made it part of their standard operating equipment. It is even used to track prisoners on day leave or parole. By the turn of the century, GPS receiving devices became more inexpensive and are now affordable for much of the public. They are standard in most new car designs and are a favorite of hunters and fishermen making long treks in the wilderness. In addition, parents can fit their children with miniature tracking devices so that they can use GPS to know where their children are at all times. While many anxious parents welcome this aspect of technology, others are already beginning to wonder if the GPS revolution is just another way for the government to infringe on its citizens' privacy.

18 In paragraph 6, why does the author mention "GPS receiving devices"?

Ⓐ To explain why they are becoming more popular than in the past

Ⓑ To show that scientists have found ways to make them less expensive

Ⓒ To highlight that many companies produce them, thereby driving prices down

Ⓓ To prove that even the poorest person can afford to purchase one

This changed in August 1973. The Department of Defense ordered Air Force Colonel Brad Parkinson to head a team to create a navigation system that all three branches of the military and civilians could utilize. ■ If anyone can be called the father of GPS, Parkinson deserves the title. ■ Putting aside service rivalries, Parkinson's team created a plan implementing aspects of all three services' systems. ■ By 1978, the system was ready and being tested, and the eventual cost of the system was four billion dollars. ■ The military, afraid that rival countries and civilians would use the system to attack the United States or for criminal purposes, installed a distortion in the GPS signal that led to a slight error in civilian GPS receivers. Military units had a way to eliminate the error. In 2000, the American president had the distortion eliminated.

19. Look at the four squares [■] that indicate where the following sentence could be added to the passage.

After the successful implementation of the GPS system, Parkinson retired from the Air Force and eventually became a professor at Stanford University.

Where would the sentence best fit?

Click on a square [■] to add the sentence to the passage.

20 Directions: An introductory sentence for a brief summary of the passage is provided below. Complete the summary by selecting the THREE answer choices that express the most important ideas of the passage. Some sentences do not belong because they express ideas that are not presented in the passage or are minor ideas in the passage. **This question is worth 2 points.**

Drag your answer choices to the spaces where they belong.
To remove an answer choice, click on it. To review the passage, click on **View Text**.

The American military played a decisive role in creating and running the Global Positioning System.

-
-
-

Answer Choices

1. The first satellite, *Sputnik*, gave a lot of people the idea to use satellites for navigation purposes.

2. GPS is used by civilians today for a wide variety of purposes.

3. GPS was initially devised as a method for the American military quickly to navigate under battlefield conditions.

4. Air Force Colonel Brad Parkinson was the team leader integral to the creation of GPS.

5. The three main American military services were rivals in the creation of GPS but settled their differences to work together.

6. Some people are worried that GPS will be used as a tool to take away individuals' privacy.

Actual Test
READING 1

08

TOEFL READING

Reading Section Directions

This section measures your ability to understand academic passages in English. You will have **35 minutes** to read and answer questions about **2 passages**. A clock at the top of the screen will show you how much time is remaining.

Most questions are worth 1 point but the last question for each passage is worth more than 1 point. The directions for the last question indicate how many points you may receive.

Some passages include a word or phrase that is **underlined** in blue. Click on the word or phrase to see a definition or an explanation.

When you want to move to the next question, click on **Next**. You may skip questions and go back to them later. If you want to return to previous questions, click on **Back**. You can click on **Review** at any time, and the review screen will show you which questions you have answered and which you have not answered. From this review screen, you may go directly to any question you have already seen in the Reading section.

Click on **Continue** to go on.

Balance in the Oceans

Various marine life

 Ocean predators come in all shapes and sizes. For example, one of the less well-known ones is the colorful starfish, which feeds on plant life, coral, or other shellfish such as mussels for sustenance. A more bloodcurdling example, especially to human beings and most other species of fish, is the shark even though most scientists agree that only ten percent of the 450 plus species of sharks have been documented as actually attacking humans. Still, there is another predator lurking invisibly in the bodies of water of the world, one which poses one of the greatest threats to all species of ocean life: bacteria. Though many types of fish are continually stalking and evading one another for survival, they all band together in an attempt to keep bacteria levels at bay in order to enable their own existence to continue.

 Bacteria play a dual role in the ecosystems of the oceans. On the one hand, they are beneficial as they stimulate plant life through food decomposition, which releases chemicals necessary for the growth of plant life. This is called nutrient recycling and helps keep the oceans alive. On the other hand, bacteria are major predators of all fish because they attack fragile, weak individuals. If they are allowed to run rampant and not kept in check, they could virtually suffocate the oceans. In water, bacteria prove to be an even greater threat than on land because as they proliferate, they reduce the oxygen levels necessary for organisms in the oceans to live. Furthermore, when fish populations become depleted due to factors like overfishing, microbes such as algae expand and threaten the fragile ecosystems of the oceans. Therefore, ocean predators play a critical role by thwarting bacteria growth and by maintaining the oceans' **equilibrium** by reducing vulnerable links in the food chain.

 In many ways, the balance within the oceans' ecosystems mirrors the human body. That is, all of their components must work in harmony for them to stay healthy, efficient, and alive. If one of them is missing or deficient, an entire system can be placed in jeopardy. In both the human body and the ocean, bacteria play a vital role because at manageable levels, they aid in protecting and cleaning each system of foreign agents that can be of harm. On the other hand, if bacteria levels increase and become out of control, they can take hold of a system, overrun it, and become debilitating. Therefore, both oceans and the human body have a kind of custodian that maintains bacteria levels. In the human body, it is called a phagocyte. Phagocytes eat sick, old, and dying cells, which are more prone to bacterial invasion, and thus keep the body healthy. Like in the human body, bacteria can prove fatal to the living organisms in the ocean.

Like phagocytes in the human body, ocean predators work as antibacterial custodians of the seas. In essence, they are the immune system and a vital link in the food chain because they remove small, injured, and sickly fish from the ocean environment before bacteria can become too comfortable and multiply. By ridding the ocean of weaker fish, predators allow the stronger ones to multiply, making their species stronger and more **resilient**. Without their services and with their declining numbers, bacteria would blossom to levels that would eventually overpower and kill even the strongest species of fish because of the depletion of their number-one source of life: all-important oxygen.

While the greatest battle in the ocean may seem on the surface to be the survival of the fittest fish, a closer look reveals something completely different: fish versus microorganisms. Clearly, most living organisms in the oceans are hunters by nature, but this way of life does not merely provide a food source for a dominant species. It also maintains a healthy level of bacteria in an ocean's ecosystem, thus ensuring the continuation of all species of life within that ecosystem. Major predators are necessary, like the antibacterial cells of the human body, to keep this delicate balance in synch. If their numbers continue to decline and humans ignore their vital role in the ocean, dire consequences will definitely result.

Glossary
equilibrium: balance
resilient: able to recover quickly

Balance in the Oceans

1 → Ocean predators come in all shapes and sizes. For example, one of the less well-known ones is the colorful starfish, which feeds on plant life, coral, or other shellfish such as mussels for sustenance. A more bloodcurdling example, especially to human beings and most other species of fish, is the shark even though most scientists agree that only ten percent of the 450 plus species of sharks have been documented as actually attacking humans. Still, there is another predator lurking invisibly in the bodies of water of the world, one which poses one of the greatest threats to all species of ocean life: bacteria. **Though many types of fish are continually stalking and evading one another for survival, they all band together in an attempt to keep bacteria levels at bay in order to enable their own existence to continue.**

1. Which of the sentences below best expresses the essential information in the highlighted sentence in the passage? *Incorrect* answer choices change the meaning in important ways or leave out essential information.
   - (A) Evasion tactics help fish escape the threats posed by an increasing number of bacteria.
   - (B) Various species of fish prey upon one another in order to lower bacteria levels in the ocean.
   - (C) High bacteria levels in the ocean help most species of fish to survive by providing them with food.
   - (D) Rivals or not, all fish help one another survive by preventing bacteria from proliferating.

2. Which of the following can be inferred from paragraph 1 about bacteria?
   - (A) They can be extremely detrimental to fish if their numbers increase.
   - (B) They are able to feed off themselves when other food sources are limited.
   - (C) They stimulate plant life, which, in turn, releases oxygen into the water.
   - (D) They present themselves in numerous shapes and forms as well as colors.

² → Bacteria play a dual role in the ecosystems of the oceans. On the one hand, they are beneficial as they stimulate plant life through food decomposition, which releases chemicals necessary for the growth of plant life. This is called nutrient recycling and helps keep the oceans alive. On the other hand, bacteria are major predators of all fish because they attack fragile, weak individuals. If they are allowed to run rampant and not kept in check, they could virtually suffocate the oceans. In water, bacteria prove to be an even greater threat than on land because as they proliferate, they reduce the oxygen levels necessary for organisms in the oceans to live. Furthermore, when fish populations become depleted due to factors like overfishing, microbes such as algae expand and threaten the fragile ecosystems of the oceans. Therefore, ocean predators play a critical role by thwarting bacteria growth and by maintaining the oceans' **equilibrium** by reducing vulnerable links in the food chain.

3 The author discusses "nutrient recycling" in paragraph 2 in order to
- Ⓐ show how bacteria act similarly in the ocean and the human body
- Ⓑ explain the different roles of nutrients and oxygen for species of fish
- Ⓒ indicate that bacteria have a positive impact in the oceans
- Ⓓ note how chemicals from bacteria are able to stimulate plant growth

4 According to paragraph 2, bacteria are dangerous to ocean life because
- Ⓐ they have the capability to attack both strong and weak fish
- Ⓑ they could monopolize the critical breathable gas in the ocean
- Ⓒ they get rid of vulnerable links, like dying fish, in the food chain
- Ⓓ they blossom out of control when overfishing becomes dominant

📖 ***Glossary***
equilibrium: balance

In many ways, the balance within the oceans' ecosystems mirrors the human body. That is, all of their components must work in harmony for them to stay healthy, efficient, and alive. If one of them is missing or deficient, an entire system can be placed in jeopardy. In both the human body and the ocean, bacteria play a vital role because at manageable levels, they aid in protecting and cleaning each system of foreign agents that can be of harm. On the other hand, if bacteria levels increase and become out of control, they can take hold of a system, overrun it, and become debilitating. Therefore, both oceans and the human body have a kind of custodian that maintains bacteria levels. In the human body, it is called a phagocyte. Phagocytes eat sick, old, and dying cells, which are more prone to bacterial invasion, and thus keep the body healthy. Like in the human body, bacteria can prove fatal to the living organisms in the ocean.

5 The word "debilitating" in the passage is closest in meaning to

Ⓐ stimulating
Ⓑ hindering
Ⓒ elevating
Ⓓ devastating

⁴ ➜ Like phagocytes in the human body, ocean predators work as antibacterial custodians of the seas. In essence, they are the immune system and a vital link in the food chain because they remove small, injured, and sickly fish from the ocean environment before bacteria can become too comfortable and multiply. By ridding the ocean of weaker fish, predators allow the stronger ones to multiply, making their species stronger and more **resilient**. Without their services and with their declining numbers, bacteria would blossom to levels that would eventually overpower and kill even the strongest species of fish because of the depletion of their number-one source of life: all-important oxygen.

6. In paragraph 4, the author's description of phagocytes mentions all of the following EXCEPT:

   A. How they help the human body
   B. How they are similar to ocean predators
   C. How they help weakened cells revive
   D. How they act as cleaning agents

7. According to paragraph 4, the elimination of weaker fish by ocean predators

   A. can often have an adverse effect on the populations of certain prey species
   B. inadvertently helps stronger species of fish proliferate more easily
   C. reduces oxygen levels, thereby causing bacteria to multiply in their prey
   D. allows bacteria to grow and multiply in the stronger individuals of a species

Glossary
resilient: able to recover quickly

■ While the greatest battle in the ocean may seem on the surface to be the survival of the fittest fish, a closer look reveals something completely different: fish versus microorganisms. ■ Clearly, most living organisms in the oceans are hunters by nature, but this way of life does not merely provide a food source for a dominant species. ■ It also maintains a healthy level of bacteria in an ocean's ecosystem, thus ensuring the continuation of all species of life within that ecosystem. ■ Major predators are necessary, like the antibacterial cells of the human body, to keep this delicate balance in synch. If their numbers continue to decline and humans ignore their vital role in the ocean, dire consequences will definitely result.

8 The word "It" in the passage refers to

- Ⓐ this way of life
- Ⓑ a food source
- Ⓒ a dominant species
- Ⓓ a healthy level of bacteria

9 Look at the four squares [■] that indicate where the following sentence could be added to the passage.

As a result, fish are doing themselves a favor in the long run by dining on one another.

Where would the sentence best fit?

Click on a square [■] to add the sentence to the passage.

10 Directions: An introductory sentence for a brief summary of the passage is provided below. Complete the summary by selecting the THREE answer choices that express the most important ideas of the passage. Some sentences do not belong because they express ideas that are not presented in the passage or are minor ideas in the passage. **This question is worth 2 points.**

Drag your answer choices to the spaces where they belong.
To remove an answer choice, click on it. To review the passage, click on **View Text**.

Bacteria are a great threat to ocean ecosystems, and without predators, they could become a serious hazard to ocean life.

-
-
-

Answer Choices

1. Extreme levels of bacteria could deplete oxygen levels in the ocean and harm fish.
2. Around ten percent of all the species of sharks have attacked humans.
3. Overfishing is one of the more serious causes of an increase in bacteria levels in the oceans.
4. Ocean predators are similar to a human's immune system because they get rid of weaker fish.
5. Phagocytes serve as important custodians of the human body by controlling bacteria levels.
6. Major ocean predators are vital because they maintain harmony in its fragile ecosystems.

Lineages

    A lineage refers to a group of people who can show they are all related to one another through a common ancestor. It can always be proven that its members share blood ties. Sometimes groups of people will claim a common ancestor but be unable to prove the connection either because the claims are rooted more in myth than in fact or because the common ancestor is believed to have existed before the advent of written records within those groups' cultures. Such groups are not considered lineages but clans. Lineages can be calculated in several different ways. Historically, the most common, especially in the West, has been to trace a person's ancestry back through the father's line. This is known as a patrilineal system of descent. Some other cultures, most notably certain Native American tribes, trace a person's ancestry back through the mother's line, which is known as a matrilineal system of descent. Occasionally, a culture traces a person's lineage through both matrilineal and patrilineal lines. This is referred to as a bilineal system of descent. In these societies, both male and female lines are considered equally valid; however, people must decide with which group of relatives they most want to be identified. Finally, it is possible for a culture to allow members to use either matrilineal or patrilineal lines of descent but not both.

    The easiest way to learn one's lineage is to look through old records of births and marriages. Government and hospital records will often serve for recent generations, but they tend to become less important as one goes further back in time. For relatives more than a century distant, church and parish records are the prime sources of information. Of course, it may not be necessary for a person to carry out all of the research on his lineage. Often, other members of a person's extended family will have carried out genealogical research in the past. Once these people have been identified as relatives, their research can be imported into the person's own work. This is especially easy today thanks to online genealogy sites, many of which allow users to search through a database of pre-researched lineages to see if their own has already been traced by someone else.

    Today, individuals, driven by an urge to learn more about their family's history or by a desire to find a connection to someone historically important, often trace their personal lineages through online genealogy sites. While this sort of amateur genealogy can be entertaining, lineages used to be far more vital to a person's social status. For example, in Victorian England, lines of descent were purely patrilineal. That meant people's relationships were traced only through the males and that the eldest males would normally be the only ones to inherit property. Similarly, patrilineal descent is often used in monarchies to determine who has the best claim on the throne. In smaller tribes, lineages are often also important in determining whom a person can marry. While virtually all cultures have rules prohibiting incest, the definition of what constitutes incest fluctuates widely once one moves beyond members of the nuclear family. For instance, certain cousins might not be considered blood relatives if descent is unilineal no matter if it is calculated from the mother's or father's line.

Lineages can also be used to unearth the common roots of various ethnic groups. In such cases, anthropologists look at something called mitochondrial DNA. This is DNA found in the mitochondria, the organelles in cells that are responsible for converting food molecules into energy. The DNA in mitochondria is different from that in the rest of human bodies and is believed to be derived from single-celled organisms which were absorbed by the cells of multicellular organisms billions of years ago. Unlike regular DNA, mitochondrial DNA is passed down exclusively from mother to child. As a result, it changes far more slowly than regular DNA, which is diluted by fifty percent each generation. This means that anthropologists can compare mitochondrial DNA to determine whether individuals share a genetic lineage. If they have samples of mitochondrial DNA from human fossils to analyze as well, they can determine when the lineage began.

Lineages

¹→ A lineage refers to a group of people who can show they are all related to one another through a common ancestor. It can always be proven that its members share blood ties. Sometimes groups of people will claim a common ancestor but be unable to prove the connection either because the claims are rooted more in myth than in fact or because the common ancestor is believed to have existed before the advent of written records within those groups' cultures. Such groups are not considered lineages but clans. Lineages can be calculated in several different ways. Historically, the most common, especially in the West, has been to trace a person's ancestry back through the father's line. This is known as a patrilineal system of descent. Some other cultures, most notably certain Native American tribes, trace a person's ancestry back through the mother's line, which is known as a matrilineal system of descent. Occasionally, a culture traces a person's lineage through both matrilineal and patrilineal lines. This is referred to as a bilineal system of descent. In these societies, both male and female lines are considered equally valid; however, people must decide with which group of relatives they most want to be identified. Finally, it is possible for a culture to allow members to use either matrilineal or patrilineal lines of descent but not both.

11 Which of the sentences below best expresses the essential information in the highlighted sentence in the passage? *Incorrect* answer choices change the meaning in important ways or leave out essential information.

Ⓐ Some people are descended from mythological figures that existed before the advent of written records or historical documents.

Ⓑ There are those who believe that myths are more important in determining descent than written or historical records are.

Ⓒ Those who make unsubstantiated claims that involve legendary figures cast doubt on the entire concept of lineages and systems of descent.

Ⓓ Some people claim they have common ancestors who are not verifiable because of their mythical or prehistoric origins.

12 The author discusses "clans" in paragraph 1 in order to

Ⓐ argue that they should be treated like lineages

Ⓑ show a weakness in the concept of lineages

Ⓒ demonstrate why anthropologists do not recognize them

Ⓓ explain a distinction made by anthropologists

2 → The easiest way to learn one's lineage is to look through old records of births and marriages. Government and hospital records will often serve for recent generations, but they tend to become less important as one goes further back in time. For relatives more than a century distant, church and parish records are the prime sources of information. Of course, it may not be necessary for a person to carry out all of the research on his lineage. Often, other members of a person's extended family will have carried out genealogical research in the past. Once these people have been identified as relatives, their research can be imported into the person's own work. This is especially easy today thanks to online genealogy sites, many of which allow users to search through a database of pre-researched lineages to see if their own has already been traced by someone else.

13 According to paragraph 2, what is a benefit of online genealogy sites?

Ⓐ They are much cheaper than hiring someone to do the research offline.

Ⓑ They allow people to see if their genealogy has already been investigated.

Ⓒ They can instantly search church and parish records for documentation of relatives.

Ⓓ They employ specially trained experts who can provide people with professional assistance.

3 → Today, individuals, driven by an urge to learn more about their family's history or by a desire to find a connection to someone historically important, often trace their personal lineages through online genealogy sites. While this sort of amateur genealogy can be entertaining, lineages used to be far more vital to a person's social status. For example, in Victorian England, lines of descent were purely patrilineal. That meant people's relationships were traced only through the males and that the eldest males would normally be the only ones to inherit property. Similarly, patrilineal descent is often used in monarchies to determine who has the best claim on the throne. In smaller tribes, lineages are often also important in determining whom a person can marry. While virtually all cultures have rules prohibiting incest, the definition of what constitutes incest fluctuates widely once one moves beyond members of the nuclear family. For instance, certain cousins might not be considered blood relatives if descent is unilineal no matter if it is calculated from the mother's or father's line.

14. According to paragraph 3, why do people today normally try to learn their lineages?
   Ⓐ To become trained amateur genealogists
   Ⓑ To satisfy their personal curiosity
   Ⓒ To avoid accidentally committing incest
   Ⓓ To see if they have the right to inherit

15. Why does the author mention "monarchies" in paragraph 3?
   Ⓐ To provide an example of an outdated mode of government
   Ⓑ To demonstrate that lineages are vital to modern societies
   Ⓒ To explain how anthropologists can trace long-lost lineages
   Ⓓ To show another way in which lineages can be important

16. The word "prohibiting" in the passage is closest in meaning to
   Ⓐ explaining
   Ⓑ condemning
   Ⓒ permitting
   Ⓓ forbidding

⁴→ Lineages can also be used to unearth the common roots of various ethnic groups. In such cases, anthropologists look at something called mitochondrial DNA. This is DNA found in the mitochondria, the organelles in cells that are responsible for converting food molecules into energy. The DNA in mitochondria is different from that in the rest of human bodies and is believed to be derived from single-celled organisms which were absorbed by the cells of multicellular organisms billions of years ago. Unlike regular DNA, mitochondrial DNA is passed down exclusively from mother to child. As a result, it changes far more slowly than regular DNA, which is diluted by fifty percent each generation. This means that anthropologists can compare mitochondrial DNA to determine whether individuals share a genetic lineage. If they have samples of mitochondrial DNA from human fossils to analyze as well, they can determine when the lineage began.

17 The word "diluted" in the passage is closest in meaning to
   Ⓐ concentrated
   Ⓑ reduced
   Ⓒ mixed
   Ⓓ disappeared

18 According to paragraph 4, how is mitochondrial DNA different from regular DNA?
   Ⓐ It is billions of years older and thousands of times more complex.
   Ⓑ It only exists in the cells of women and children.
   Ⓒ It is only passed on through matrilineal lines.
   Ⓓ It can replicate itself without ever suffering from mutations.

Lineages can also be used to unearth the common roots of various ethnic groups. In such cases, anthropologists look at something called mitochondrial DNA. This is DNA found in the mitochondria, the organelles in cells that are responsible for converting food molecules into energy. The DNA in mitochondria is different from that in the rest of human bodies and is believed to be derived from single-celled organisms which were absorbed by the cells of multicellular organisms billions of years ago. Unlike regular DNA, mitochondrial DNA is passed down exclusively from mother to child. As a result, it changes far more slowly than regular DNA, which is diluted by fifty percent each generation. This means that anthropologists can compare mitochondrial DNA to determine whether individuals share a genetic lineage. If they have samples of mitochondrial DNA from human fossils to analyze as well, they can determine when the lineage began.

19 Look at the four squares [■] that indicate where the following sentence could be added to the passage.

This normally requires tracing people's lines back much further than historical records allow.

Where would the sentence best fit?

Click on a square [■] to add the sentence to the passage.

20 Directions: An introductory sentence for a brief summary of the passage is provided below. Complete the summary by selecting the THREE answer choices that express the most important ideas of the passage. Some sentences do not belong because they express ideas that are not presented in the passage or are minor ideas in the passage. **This question is worth 2 points.**

Drag your answer choices to the spaces where they belong.
To remove an answer choice, click on it. To review the passage, click on **View Text**.

Lineage has been important historically, and while not as important today, many people still attempt to determine their own lineage.

-
-
-

Answer Choices

1. In the past, patrilineal relationships often determined who would inherit powerful positions or family wealth.

2. Mitochondrial DNA is of little use in allowing scientists to determine the shared genetic lineages of various people.

3. When trying to determine one's own lineage, the majority of people have to search through various church records.

4. If people are unable to determine their relationships with others, there is a high probability that they may commit incest.

5. Most of the people trying to determine their family history do so out of curiosity and a wish to know who their ancestors were.

6. While many cultures have traced their ancestry through males, there have been some that are matrilineal and therefore focus on relationships through mothers.

How to Master Skills for the TOEFL® iBT

Actual Test
READING 1

09

TOEFL READING

Reading Section Directions

This section measures your ability to understand academic passages in English. You will have **35 minutes** to read and answer questions about **2 passages**. A clock at the top of the screen will show you how much time is remaining.

Most questions are worth 1 point but the last question for each passage is worth more than 1 point. The directions for the last question indicate how many points you may receive.

Some passages include a word or phrase that is **underlined** in blue. Click on the word or phrase to see a definition or an explanation.

When you want to move to the next question, click on **Next**. You may skip questions and go back to them later. If you want to return to previous questions, click on **Back**. You can click on **Review** at any time, and the review screen will show you which questions you have answered and which you have not answered. From this review screen, you may go directly to any question you have already seen in the Reading section.

Click on **Continue** to go on.

The Nitrogen Cycle

A number of gases can be found in the Earth's atmosphere. Oxygen comprises roughly twenty percent of the atmosphere while argon makes up around one percent. There are smaller amounts of gases such as carbon dioxide, helium, methane, and neon. By far the largest percentage of the atmosphere is comprised of the gas nitrogen, which makes up approximately seventy-eight percent of the planet's atmosphere. Nitrogen is actually an invaluable gas for life on the planet and often converts into different forms. These transformations, which consist of five parts, are collectively known as the nitrogen cycle.

Nitrogen is vital both to plants and animals. For instance, plants require nitrogen to create **chlorophyll**, which is utilized in the process of **photosynthesis**, from which plants obtain both food and energy. As for animals, nitrogen is necessary for amino acids, proteins, and DNA and is part of various cells in the bodies of animals, including humans. Unfortunately, the nitrogen that exists in the atmosphere, called N_2, is inert and does not readily combine with other elements. The types of nitrogen which are required by plants and animals are nitrate (NO_3) and nitrite (NO_2), both of which combine nitrogen and oxygen, and ammonium (NH_4), a combination of nitrogen and four hydrogen atoms.

It is bacteria that enable nitrogen to combine with other elements to put nitrogen into forms that can be utilized by plants and animals. This happens during the first stage of the nitrogen cycle, which is called fixation. Diazotrophs are nitrogen-fixing bacteria in the soil that contain an enzyme known as nitrogenase. It is this enzyme that permits nitrogen to combine with hydrogen to form ammonia, but this can only happen when there is no oxygen present. A benefit of ammonia is that it dissolves in water, so plant and animal enzymes can interact with it more easily.

The second part of the cycle is called nitrification and happens when bacteria transform ammonia into nitrate. There are two steps in the process, and each is performed by a different type of bacteria. What happens is that one type of soil bacteria, such as *Nitrosomonas*, transforms ammonia into nitrite. After that, *Nitrobacter*, a different kind of soil bacteria, creates nitrate by adding a third oxygen molecule. Interestingly, lightning strikes and volcanic eruptions are so powerful that they are capable of transforming N_2 into NO_2; however, this happens on a relatively small scale and is not sufficient to create enough nitrite and nitrate for plants.

Assimilation is the third part of the nitrogen cycle and happens when plants use their roots to absorb nitrates from the soil. The plants then utilize the nitrates to make amino acids, nucleic acids, and other various chemicals that are required for them to live. An additional advantage is that many animals consume these plants and can then utilize the amino acids and nucleic acids for themselves.

At various times, plants and animals die, and that results in the fourth stage of the nitrogen cycle, which is known as ammonification, taking place. As the plants and animals decompose, certain bacteria in the soil break down the amino acids and the nucleic acids in their bodies and transform them back to nitrates and ammonia. Sometimes the nitrates and the ammonia remain in the soil and are once again changed into forms that can be used by plants. Other times, the ammonia may be changed so that it reenters the atmosphere. This happens in the fifth and final stage and is important since the atmosphere has a finite amount of nitrogen. Were the nitrogen to remain in the soil and not return to the atmosphere, there would be tremendous changes to the Earth's entire ecosystem.

The fifth stage, called denitrification, happens due to the actions of anaerobic bacteria, which are bacteria that are active only when there is no oxygen. Denitrification usually happens deep underground or in places with lots of mud, such as swamps, marshes, and bogs. The bacteria take the excess nitrogen in the soil, convert it into N_2, and release it back into the atmosphere. This prevents nitrogen levels in the soil from becoming too high, replenishes the supply of nitrogen in the atmosphere, and completes the nitrogen cycle.

Glossary

chlorophyll: a green pigment found in the leaves of plants and that helps with photosynthesis

photosynthesis: the process through which plants use water and carbon dioxide to create oxygen and energy for themselves

The Nitrogen Cycle

¹→ A number of gases can be found in the Earth's atmosphere. Oxygen comprises roughly twenty percent of the atmosphere while argon makes up around one percent. There are smaller amounts of gases such as carbon dioxide, helium, methane, and neon. By far the largest percentage of the atmosphere is comprised of the gas nitrogen, which makes up approximately seventy-eight percent of the planet's atmosphere. Nitrogen is actually an invaluable gas for life on the planet and often converts into different forms. These transformations, which consist of five parts, are collectively known as the nitrogen cycle.

1. In paragraph 1, the author's description of nitrogen mentions which of the following?
   - Ⓐ How much of the atmosphere it makes up
   - Ⓑ Which part of the atmosphere it is usually found in
   - Ⓒ How it can combine with oxygen and other elements
   - Ⓓ What changes it goes through in the nitrogen cycle

2 → Nitrogen is vital both to plants and animals. For instance, plants require nitrogen to create **chlorophyll**, which is utilized in the process of **photosynthesis**, from which plants obtain both food and energy. As for animals, nitrogen is necessary for amino acids, proteins, and DNA and is part of various cells in the bodies of animals, including humans. Unfortunately, the nitrogen that exists in the atmosphere, called N_2, is inert and does not readily combine with other elements. The types of nitrogen which are required by plants and animals are nitrate (NO_3) and nitrite (NO_2), both of which combine nitrogen and oxygen, and ammonium (NH_4), a combination of nitrogen and four hydrogen atoms.

2. In paragraph 2, the author implies that nitrogen

  Ⓐ is not needed by a large number of plants and animals
  Ⓑ is necessary for plants to create food for themselves
  Ⓒ is unable to create compounds with other elements
  Ⓓ is directly involved in the process of photosynthesis

Glossary

chlorophyll: a green pigment found in the leaves of plants and that helps with photosynthesis

photosynthesis: the process through which plants use water and carbon dioxide to create oxygen and energy for themselves

³ → It is bacteria that enable nitrogen to combine with other elements to put nitrogen into forms that can be utilized by plants and animals. This happens during the first stage of the nitrogen cycle, which is called fixation. Diazotrophs are nitrogen-fixing bacteria in the soil that contain an enzyme known as nitrogenase. It is this enzyme that permits nitrogen to combine with hydrogen to form ammonia, but this can only happen when there is no oxygen present. A benefit of ammonia is that it dissolves in water, so plant and animal enzymes can interact with it more easily.

⁴ → The second part of the cycle is called nitrification and happens when bacteria transform ammonia into nitrate. There are two steps in the process, and each is performed by a different type of bacteria. What happens is that one type of soil bacteria, such as *Nitrosomonas*, transforms ammonia into nitrite. After that, *Nitrobacter*, a different kind of soil bacteria, creates nitrate by adding a third oxygen molecule. Interestingly, lightning strikes and volcanic eruptions are so powerful that they are capable of transforming N_2 into NO_2; however, this happens on a relatively small scale and is not sufficient to create enough nitrite and nitrate for plants.

3. In paragraph 3, the author uses "Diazotrophs" as an example of
  Ⓐ elements that are able to combine with nitrogen to form compounds
  Ⓑ bacteria that are commonly found in the compound ammonia
  Ⓒ enzymes that help nitrogenase let oxygen combine with nitrogen
  Ⓓ organisms that are involved in the stage called nitrogen fixation

4. In paragraph 4, why does the author mention "lightning strikes and volcanic eruptions"?
  Ⓐ To show two ways in which nitrite can be formed by nature
  Ⓑ To claim that they are some of nature's most powerful forces
  Ⓒ To point out that plants are capable of benefitting from them
  Ⓓ To note that they can act in the same way as *Nitrosomonas*

5. In paragraph 4, all of the following questions are answered EXCEPT:
  Ⓐ How are *Nitrosomonas* and *Nitrobacter* similar to each other?
  Ⓑ What is the name of the second stage of the nitrogen cycle?
  Ⓒ Where in the world do the most lightning strikes hit the ground?
  Ⓓ How is ammonia changed into nitrate in the nitrogen cycle?

Assimilation is the third part of the nitrogen cycle and happens when plants use their roots to absorb nitrates from the soil. The plants then utilize the nitrates to make amino acids, nucleic acids, and other various chemicals that are required for them to live. An additional advantage is that many animals consume these plants and can then utilize the amino acids and nucleic acids for themselves.

At various times, plants and animals die, and that results in the fourth stage of the nitrogen cycle, which is known as ammonification, taking place. As the plants and animals decompose, certain bacteria in the soil break down the amino acids and the nucleic acids in their bodies and transform them back to nitrates and ammonia. Sometimes the nitrates and the ammonia remain in the soil and are once again changed into forms that can be used by plants. Other times, the ammonia may be changed so that it reenters the atmosphere. This happens in the fifth and final stage and is important since the atmosphere has a finite amount of nitrogen. Were the nitrogen to remain in the soil and not return to the atmosphere, there would be tremendous changes to the Earth's entire ecosystem.

6 Which of the sentences below best expresses the essential information in the highlighted sentence in the passage? *Incorrect* answer choices change the meaning in important ways or leave out essential information.

Ⓐ Animals get enough amino and nucleic acids by consuming certain types of plants.
Ⓑ Animals benefit by eating the plants and then using the various acids in them.
Ⓒ It is not possible for animals to make some acids, so they have to eat lots of plants.
Ⓓ Many plants make amino and nucleic acids, which animals then consume.

7 The word "finite" in the passage is closest in meaning to

Ⓐ valuable
Ⓑ considerable
Ⓒ limited
Ⓓ excessive

⁷ ➜ The fifth stage, called denitrification, happens due to the actions of anaerobic bacteria, which are bacteria that are active only when there is no oxygen. Denitrification usually happens deep underground or in places with lots of mud, such as swamps, marshes, and bogs. The bacteria take the excess nitrogen in the soil, convert it into N_2, and release it back into the atmosphere. This prevents nitrogen levels in the soil from becoming too high, replenishes the supply of nitrogen in the atmosphere, and completes the nitrogen cycle.

8. According to paragraph 7, which of the following is true of denitrification?

   Ⓐ It involves moving nitrogen from the air to the soil.
   Ⓑ It needs to happen in areas that have a lack of oxygen.
   Ⓒ It helps reduce the amount of nitrogen in the air.
   Ⓓ It can be done by any type of bacteria in the soil.

At various times, plants and animals die, and that results in the fourth stage of the nitrogen cycle, which is known as ammonification, taking place. As the plants and animals decompose, certain bacteria in the soil break down the amino acids and the nucleic acids in their bodies and transform them back to nitrates and ammonia. Sometimes the nitrates and the ammonia remain in the soil and are once again changed into forms that can be used by plants. ■ Other times, the ammonia may be changed so that it reenters the atmosphere. ■ This happens in the fifth and final stage and is important since the atmosphere has a finite amount of nitrogen. ■ Were the nitrogen to remain in the soil and not return to the atmosphere, there would be tremendous changes to the Earth's entire ecosystem. ■

9 Look at the four squares [■] that indicate where the following sentence could be added to the passage.

Which of these actions take place frequently depends on the type of bacteria acting on the nitrates and the ammonia.

Where would the sentence best fit?

Click on a square [■] to add the sentence to the passage.

10 Directions: An introductory sentence for a brief summary of the passage is provided below. Complete the summary by selecting the THREE answer choices that express the most important ideas of the passage. Some sentences do not belong because they express ideas that are not presented in the passage or are minor ideas in the passage. **This question is worth 2 points.**

Drag your answer choices to the spaces where they belong.
To remove an answer choice, click on it. To review the passage, click on **View Text**.

The nitrogen cycle shows how nitrogen changes forms while moving from the air to the ground.

-
-
-

Answer Choices

1. Special types of bacteria are needed for nitrogen to change forms.
2. Plants and animals benefit when nitrogen combines with other elements.
3. Some natural phenomena can change nitrogen into nitrite.
4. Nitrogen is necessary for plants to create chlorophyll, which helps them get energy.
5. The stages of the cycle help maintain the nitrogen supply in the air and the soil.
6. Nitrogen does not easily combine with other elements like oxygen and hydrogen.

The Whooping Crane

Whooping cranes in a winter habitat

    The whooping crane is a grand migratory waterfowl native only to North America. Its features are striking as a mature whooping crane is all white and stands five feet tall with a wingspan of about eight feet. Its head is colored red and black, and its eyes are a deep golden hue. Unfortunately, by the late 1930s, the whooping crane was on the verge of extinction as fewer than twenty-five remained in the wild. Previously, wild flocks spent the warmer parts of the year in their native habitat of northern Canada, and, around August, they made the 2,500-mile southerly journey to the gulf coast of Texas in the United States. Today, only one flock remains in the wild, and it consists of about 150 to 200 whooping cranes. Continuing conservationist efforts are attempting to increase its populations, which face, as they traditionally have, an uphill battle by introducing new habitats and educational methods of migration.

    There are two major factors which contributed to the decline of the whooping crane in the early twentieth century. First, they were originally hunted by people for food as well as their beautiful feathers, which were used to adorn luxurious clothing and other fashionable items. Second, their natural habitat wetlands were beginning to dry up due to agricultural exploitation and development. Thirdly, which perhaps had the most dramatic effect, was the fact that the eggs of the whooping crane were prized by collectors. Once the eggs were **pillaged** from nests, future generations became placed even more in jeopardy. Fortunately, the whooping crane, like other endangered species such as the bald eagle, ultimately became a protected species by federal law. The issue has now become how to increase their numbers back to comfortable levels.

    One method that conservationists have found some success with has been raising whooping cranes in newly established habitats in captivity and later releasing them into the wild. Two such areas have been established in Wisconsin and Florida, where eggs are placed in incubators, hatched, continually monitored, and eventually raised by specialists. Of course, the ultimate goal is to allow the whooping crane to multiply and proliferate naturally. While conservationists have been successful in increasing whooping cranes' numbers, once they are released, they are again prone to danger mainly due to the fact that when the cold winter months come, they lack the immediate ability to migrate to the south because, in essence, most of them are orphans. Additionally, during frigid seasons, food sources become scarce, and migration to more fertile feeding grounds becomes mandatory for their survival. Migration, then, is the second major hurdle whooping cranes and conservationists alike need to overcome to secure the birds' perpetuation.

The main issue is that migration is learned from the young chick's parents, and in most cases, whooping cranes born in captivity have none. Still, like all migratory birds, they have a natural instinct called imprinting. This means they will follow and trust the first object they open their eyes to. This theory laid the groundwork for the conservationists' imaginative plan of aircraft-led migration. Humans act like parents with ultralight aircraft and allow young whooping cranes to imprint on them as if they were their natural parents. Even before they are born, the chicks are exposed to airplane sounds when they are still in their eggs. Later, they follow the small planes around on the taxiways and finally go on training flights in the air to build strength and experience. Through this process, conservationists instill in whooping cranes a natural sense of migration. Once the birds are mature enough, the small planes lead the flock from Wisconsin to their wintering habitat in Florida.

So far, airplane-led migration has been a huge success. Without it, the whooping cranes would succumb to the harsh winters of Wisconsin and die. But with the aid of humans, they have migrated the 1,250 miles from north to south with few hitches. Once the birds become more educated and confident, they are allowed to follow their imprinted instincts and migrate without human aid. Without alternative methods of human intervention, the whooping cranes could find themselves lost forever as just another extinction statistic.

Glossary
pillaged: stolen; plundered

The Whooping Crane

1 → The whooping crane is a grand migratory waterfowl native only to North America. Its features are striking as a mature whooping crane is all white and stands five feet tall with a wingspan of about eight feet. Its head is colored red and black, and its eyes are a deep golden hue. Unfortunately, by the late 1930s, the whooping crane was on the verge of extinction as fewer than twenty-five remained in the wild. Previously, wild flocks spent the warmer parts of the year in their native habitat of northern Canada, and, around August, they made the 2,500-mile southerly journey to the gulf coast of Texas in the United States. Today, only one flock remains in the wild, and it consists of about 150 to 200 whooping cranes. Continuing conservationist efforts are attempting to increase its populations, which face, as they traditionally have, an uphill battle by introducing new habitats and educational methods of migration.

11 According to paragraph 1, which of the following is true of the whooping crane?

- (A) The features of the waterfowl allow it to blend in with its habitat.
- (B) It became an endangered species in the late twentieth century.
- (C) The wild flocks have many different habitats in North America.
- (D) It is indigenous to two countries, the United States and Canada.

2 → There are two major factors which contributed to the decline of the whooping crane in the early twentieth century. First, they were originally hunted by people for food as well as their beautiful feathers, which were used to adorn luxurious clothing and other fashionable items. Second, their natural habitat wetlands were beginning to dry up due to agricultural exploitation and development. Thirdly, which perhaps had the most dramatic effect, was the fact that the eggs of the whooping crane were prized by collectors. Once the eggs were **pillaged** from nests, future generations became placed even more in jeopardy. Fortunately, the whooping crane, like other endangered species such as the bald eagle, ultimately became a protected species by federal law. The issue has now become how to increase their numbers back to comfortable levels.

12. According to paragraph 2, which of the following is NOT true of the dangers whooping cranes have faced?

   (A) They were killed for their feathers, which were used for luxury items.
   (B) Their eggs were stolen from nests for the benefit of collectors.
   (C) They lost many of their habitats due to farmland expansion.
   (D) They were hunted for sport by people due to their great size.

Glossary
pillaged: stolen; plundered

³ ➔ One method that conservationists have found some success with has been raising whooping cranes in newly established habitats in captivity and later releasing them into the wild. Two such areas have been established in Wisconsin and Florida, where eggs are placed in incubators, hatched, continually monitored, and eventually raised by specialists. Of course, the ultimate goal is to allow the whooping crane to multiply and proliferate naturally. While conservationists have been successful in increasing whooping cranes' numbers, once they are released, they are again prone to danger mainly due to the fact that when the cold winter months come, they lack the immediate ability to migrate to the south because, in essence, most of them are orphans. Additionally, during frigid seasons, food sources become scarce, and migration to more fertile feeding grounds becomes mandatory for their survival. Migration, then, is the second major hurdle whooping cranes and conservationists alike need to overcome to secure the birds' perpetuation.

13 Which of the sentences below best expresses the essential information in the highlighted sentence in the passage? *Incorrect* answer choices change the meaning in important ways or leave out essential information.

Ⓐ Whooping cranes raised by humans face problems when they need to migrate to the south because they have no parental guidance.

Ⓑ Many whooping cranes freeze to death because they have no parents to keep them warm or to feed them during their migration to the south.

Ⓒ Conservationists have overlooked the fact that the increase in populations means nothing if the whooping cranes cannot migrate to the south.

Ⓓ The most critical need is to formulate some new method of migration once the whooping cranes are released from captivity.

14 According to paragraph 3, why is it so important for birds such as the whooping crane to migrate?

Ⓐ It allows them to interact with other individuals and to diversify their flocks.

Ⓑ It provides them with ample food sources, which become scarce in the winter.

Ⓒ It takes them to a warm habitat, where they will mate and produce offspring.

Ⓓ It fulfills their intrinsic need annually to move from one habitat to another.

⁴ ➡ The main issue is that migration is learned from the young chick's parents, and in most cases, whooping cranes born in captivity have none. Still, like all migratory birds, they have a natural instinct called imprinting. This means they will follow and trust the first object they open their eyes to. This theory laid the groundwork for the conservationists' imaginative plan of aircraft-led migration. Humans act like parents with ultralight aircraft and allow young whooping cranes to imprint on them as if they were their natural parents. Even before they are born, the chicks are exposed to airplane sounds when they are still in their eggs. Later, they follow the small planes around on the taxiways and finally go on training flights in the air to build strength and experience. Through this process, conservationists instill in whooping cranes a natural sense of migration. Once the birds are mature enough, the small planes lead the flock from Wisconsin to their wintering habitat in Florida.

15 The author discusses "imprinting" in paragraph 4 in order to
  Ⓐ reveal the natural instincts singularly associated with the whooping crane
  Ⓑ contrast the whooping crane with other waterfowl in their migratory desires
  Ⓒ provide the basis for the idea of using airplanes to lead migrating birds
  Ⓓ note that imprinting has very little to do with a bird's ability to migrate

16 The word "they" in the passage refers to
  Ⓐ the young chick's parents
  Ⓑ most cases
  Ⓒ whooping cranes
  Ⓓ all migratory birds

17 According to paragraph 4, what premise makes airplane-led migration work?
  Ⓐ Whooping cranes mistake the ultralight planes as leaders and follow them.
  Ⓑ Young cranes think the sound of a plane is the call of their mother.
  Ⓒ Humans can condition the cranes to believe airplanes are their parents.
  Ⓓ Imprinting is bypassed and replaced with humans as surrogate parents.

So far, airplane-led migration has been a huge success. Without it, the whooping cranes would succumb to the harsh winters of Wisconsin and die. But with the aid of humans, they have migrated the 1,250 miles from north to south with few hitches. Once the birds become more educated and confident, they are allowed to follow their imprinted instincts and migrate without human aid. Without alternative methods of human intervention, the whooping cranes could find themselves lost forever as just another extinction statistic.

18 The word "hitches" in the passage is closest in meaning to

Ⓐ stops
Ⓑ complaints
Ⓒ diversions
Ⓓ difficulties

There are two major factors which contributed to the decline of the whooping crane in the early twentieth century. First, they were originally hunted by people for food as well as their beautiful feathers, which were used to adorn luxurious clothing and other fashionable items. Second, their natural habitat wetlands were beginning to dry up due to agricultural exploitation and development. Thirdly, which perhaps had the most dramatic effect, was the fact that the eggs of the whooping crane were prized by collectors. ■1 Once the eggs were **pillaged** from nests, future generations became placed even more in jeopardy. ■2 Fortunately, the whooping crane, like other endangered species such as the bald eagle, ultimately became a protected species by federal law. ■3 The issue has now become how to increase their numbers back to comfortable levels. ■4

19 Look at the four squares [■] that indicate where the following sentence could be added to the passage.

For instance, stiff penalties are handed down to those who tamper with the nesting area of a whooping crane.

Where would the sentence best fit?

Click on a square [■] to add the sentence to the passage.

Glossary
pillaged: stolen; plundered

20 **Directions:** An introductory sentence for a brief summary of the passage is provided below. Complete the summary by selecting the THREE answer choices that express the most important ideas of the passage. Some sentences do not belong because they express ideas that are not presented in the passage or are minor ideas in the passage. **This question is worth 2 points.**

Drag your answer choices to the spaces where they belong.
To remove an answer choice, click on it. To review the passage, click on **View Text**.

The endangered whooping crane is beginning to make a comeback thanks to the efforts of conservationists.

-
-
-

Answer Choices

1. The color of the whooping crane's eyes is deep gold, and its body is white.
2. Conservationists use the cranes' natural instincts to help them migrate.
3. There are only around two hundred or so whooping cranes left in the wild.
4. The cranes' beautiful feathers were once used to make fashionable high-end clothes.
5. Newly established habitats have been successful at increasing crane populations.
6. Airplane-led migration will hopefully allow the cranes to be self-reliant one day.

Actual Test
READING 1

10

TOEFL READING

Reading Section Directions

This section measures your ability to understand academic passages in English. You will have **35 minutes** to read and answer questions about **2 passages**. A clock at the top of the screen will show you how much time is remaining.

Most questions are worth 1 point but the last question for each passage is worth more than 1 point. The directions for the last question indicate how many points you may receive.

Some passages include a word or phrase that is **underlined** in blue. Click on the word or phrase to see a definition or an explanation.

When you want to move to the next question, click on **Next**. You may skip questions and go back to them later. If you want to return to previous questions, click on **Back**. You can click on **Review** at any time, and the review screen will show you which questions you have answered and which you have not answered. From this review screen, you may go directly to any question you have already seen in the Reading section.

Click on **Continue** to go on.

Hurricane Forces

Hurricane Isaac captured from space

 Hurricanes are some of the most destructive natural forces on the face of the entire planet. By definition, they are also known as tropical cyclones. They manifest themselves in the warm waters of the Atlantic Ocean and the eastern Pacific Ocean, usually in the form of a low-pressure weather system. Due to minimal high atmospheric winds, those near the surface of the water begin to spin and spiral in a counterclockwise direction, feeding on the heat from the ocean. With increased rotation, more water is absorbed into the system and is then released in the form of showers and thunderstorms. Once the system becomes stronger and more defined and sustained winds eclipse speeds of seventy-five miles per hour, the storm can then be classified as a true hurricane. They pose the greatest threat to human populations when they track eastward to the tepid waters of the Gulf of Mexico, where the islands of the Caribbean and the flats of the southeastern United States lie **vulnerable** to their paths of destruction, which is usually determined by two major factors: storm surge and movement.

 While high winds are commonly associated with the perils of hurricanes, the most destructive factor is the accompanying storm surge as it strikes land. Still, the torrential rains and the heavy winds a hurricane brings contribute to its storm surge, yet this occurs in a more indirect way than was previously thought. As a hurricane approaches land, water levels increase, and water is pushed onto and through the shoreline, causing major destruction. The size of the surge itself is determined by the slope of the shore, called the continental shelf, out into the ocean. If the slope is steep, the storm surge will not be as great as when it is shallower, which causes a more powerful surge due to the fact that the ocean's depth is not great enough to absorb the energy and the massive amounts of water. In fact, scientists have pointed out that one cubic yard of it weighs about 1,700 pounds.

Millions of cubic yards of surge can occur from one single storm, which, naturally, is capable of causing a catastrophic amount of damage.

Another major contributor to the measure of destruction that is caused is the movement of a hurricane. The speed of a hurricane as it makes landfall and moves inland is a major deciding factor for the extent of the damage it causes. Fast-moving hurricanes can often seem a blessing to the people and communities involved because their high speeds mean they will move on and away quickly, so they will not have a chance to dump as much water on the immediate area. However, lazy storms, and especially storms that stall on the coastline, become cyclones of devastation. Because they move so slowly or even not at all and are able to sit spinning and reenergizing themselves from the ocean, torrential rains, winds, and flooding increase, and the storm surge becomes a perpetual battering ram of destruction. However, the power of a hurricane becomes immediately diminished once over land because it is disconnected from its warm water energy source, but this does not mean it is dead by any means.

When it comes to hurricanes, direct wind destruction is a secondary worry compared to storm surge, the speed of the hurricanes' tracks, and the flooding that is associated with them. The shallow continental shelf underlying the Atlantic Ocean and the Gulf of Mexico south of the southeastern United States coupled with the low-lying landmass makes the area a prime region for disasters in the form of storm surges and flooding. This, along with the fickle nature of hurricanes and the inability of experts accurately to predict a hurricane's landfall, adds to the turmoil that hurricanes inflict on the populations of the areas they hit. Not necessarily wind, but water, remains the worst effect a hurricane can have as it is able to flood not only the immediate area where the hurricane strikes but hundreds and hundreds of miles in any given direction as well, affecting people, homes, and businesses far and wide of its main path.

Glossary
vulnerable: without protection; easily harmed

Hurricane Forces

1 → Hurricanes are some of the most destructive natural forces on the face of the entire planet. By definition, they are also known as tropical cyclones. They manifest themselves in the warm waters of the Atlantic Ocean and the eastern Pacific Ocean, usually in the form of a low-pressure weather system. Due to minimal high atmospheric winds, those near the surface of the water begin to spin and spiral in a counterclockwise direction, feeding on the heat from the ocean. With increased rotation, more water is absorbed into the system and is then released in the form of showers and thunderstorms. Once the system becomes stronger and more defined and sustained winds eclipse speeds of seventy-five miles per hour, the storm can then be classified as a true hurricane. They pose the greatest threat to human populations when they track eastward to the tepid waters of the Gulf of Mexico, where the islands of the Caribbean and the flats of the southeastern United States lie **vulnerable** to their paths of destruction, which is usually determined by two major factors: storm surge and movement.

Glossary
vulnerable: without protection; easily harmed

---

1 The word "eclipse" in the passage is closest in meaning to

- Ⓐ exceed
- Ⓑ shadow
- Ⓒ propel
- Ⓓ maintain

2 According to paragraph 1, which of the following is true of hurricanes?

- Ⓐ Storms are classified as hurricanes when gusts reach seventy-five miles per hour.
- Ⓑ One of the most defining characteristics of a hurricane is its eye.
- Ⓒ The lack of winds aloft contributes to the formation of hurricanes.
- Ⓓ They are only able to form in tropical waters near the equator.

3 Which of the following can be inferred from paragraph 1 about hurricane formation?

- Ⓐ They usually tend to twirl and spin in a clockwise direction.
- Ⓑ They are fueled by the warm waters of the Pacific Ocean.
- Ⓒ They are spawned by violent thunderstorms and wind shear.
- Ⓓ They are not likely to occur in cool oceanic areas.

2 → While high winds are commonly associated with the perils of hurricanes, the most destructive factor is the accompanying storm surge as it strikes land. Still, the torrential rains and the heavy winds a hurricane brings contribute to its storm surge, yet this occurs in a more indirect way than was previously thought. As a hurricane approaches land, water levels increase, and water is pushed onto and through the shoreline, causing major destruction. The size of the surge itself is determined by the slope of the shore, called the continental shelf, out into the ocean. If the slope is steep, the storm surge will not be as great as when it is shallower, which causes a more powerful surge due to the fact that the ocean's depth is not great enough to absorb the energy and the massive amounts of water. In fact, scientists have pointed out that one cubic yard of it weighs about 1,700 pounds. Millions of cubic yards of surge can occur from one single storm, which, naturally, is capable of causing a catastrophic amount of damage.

4. According to paragraph 2, what contributes to the destruction of storm surge?

   Ⓐ The sizes of the waves are a principal factor in the resulting damage.
   Ⓑ The contour of the ocean floor is a major determiner of its size.
   Ⓒ The torrential rains contained in a hurricane directly affect the surge.
   Ⓓ The weight of the water will destroy anything in its immediate path.

³→ Another major contributor to the measure of destruction that is caused is the movement of a hurricane. The speed of a hurricane as it makes landfall and moves inland is a major deciding factor for the extent of the damage it causes. Fast-moving hurricanes can often seem a blessing to the people and communities involved because their high speeds mean they will move on and away quickly, so they will not have a chance to dump as much water on the immediate area. However, lazy storms, and especially storms that stall on the coastline, become cyclones of devastation. Because they move so slowly or even not at all and are able to sit spinning and reenergizing themselves from the ocean, torrential rains, winds, and flooding increase, and the storm surge becomes a perpetual battering ram of destruction. However, the power of a hurricane becomes immediately diminished once over land because it is disconnected from its warm water energy source, but this does not mean it is dead by any means.

5. The author discusses "the movement of the hurricane" in paragraph 3 in order to
   Ⓐ downplay the factors of velocity and directional momentum in a hurricane
   Ⓑ show that a hurricane's tracking speed determines the amount of destruction
   Ⓒ suggest hurricanes are capable of moving in any direction at any time
   Ⓓ indicate that slow-moving storms allow people more time to seek safety

6. According to paragraph 3, which of the following is NOT true of the major forces of a hurricane?
   Ⓐ Strong winds and rain add to its storm surge.
   Ⓑ Flooding is usually much more destructive than winds.
   Ⓒ Fast-moving hurricanes ironically help lessen damage.
   Ⓓ All coastlines are affected by its storm surge.

4 ➜ When it comes to hurricanes, direct wind destruction is a secondary worry compared to storm surge, the speed of the hurricanes' tracks, and the flooding that is associated with them. The shallow continental shelf underlying the Atlantic Ocean and the Gulf of Mexico south of the southeastern United States coupled with the low-lying landmass makes the area a prime region for disasters in the form of storm surges and flooding. This, along with the fickle nature of hurricanes and the inability of experts accurately to predict a hurricane's landfall, adds to the turmoil that hurricanes inflict on the populations of the areas they hit. Not necessarily wind, but water, remains the worst effect a hurricane can have as it is able to flood not only the immediate area where the hurricane strikes but hundreds and hundreds of miles in any given direction as well, affecting people, homes, and businesses far and wide of its main path.

7. Which of the sentences below best expresses the essential information in the highlighted sentence in the passage? *Incorrect* answer choices change the meaning in important ways or leave out essential information.

   Ⓐ Flooding, which causes havoc in a very wide range of areas, is the most destructive factor of a hurricane.

   Ⓑ Wind and rain damage people, homes, and businesses every time a hurricane strikes a certain area.

   Ⓒ Cities in the direct path of a hurricane suffer the brunt of its power through flooding while the wind does little damage.

   Ⓓ Water levels do the most destruction hundreds of miles inside the hurricane, where the hurricane affects the most people.

8. According to paragraph 4, which of the following is true of a hurricane's winds?

   Ⓐ No other force of a hurricane can inflict more punishment than wind.

   Ⓑ Their destruction is short lived, unlike the effects of major floods.

   Ⓒ The direction of the winds, not their speed, is their most dangerous aspect.

   Ⓓ Low-lying areas are more prone to wind forces than elevated areas.

While high winds are commonly associated with the perils of hurricanes, the most destructive factor is the accompanying storm surge as it strikes land. ■ Still, the torrential rains and the heavy winds a hurricane brings contribute to its storm surge, yet this occurs in a more indirect way than was previously thought. ■ As a hurricane approaches land, water levels increase, and water is pushed onto and through the shoreline, causing major destruction. ■ The size of the surge itself is determined by the slope of the shore, called the continental shelf, out into the ocean. ■ If the slope is steep, the storm surge will not be as great as when it is shallower, which causes a more powerful surge due to the fact that the ocean's depth is not great enough to absorb the energy and the massive amounts of water. In fact, scientists have pointed out that one cubic yard of it weighs about 1,700 pounds. Millions of cubic yards of surge can occur from one single storm, which, naturally, is capable of causing a catastrophic amount of damage.

9. Look at the four squares [■] that indicate where the following sentence could be added to the passage.

Additionally, high tides will increase the size and potency of the storm surge from hurricanes.

Where would the sentence best fit?

Click on a square [■] to add the sentence to the passage.

10 Directions: An introductory sentence for a brief summary of the passage is provided below. Complete the summary by selecting the THREE answer choices that express the most important ideas of the passage. Some sentences do not belong because they express ideas that are not presented in the passage or are minor ideas in the passage. **This question is worth 2 points.**

Drag your answer choices to the spaces where they belong.
To remove an answer choice, click on it. To review the passage, click on **View Text**.

Two of the most defining points of destruction unleashed by a hurricane are its directional speed and storm surge.

-
-
-

Answer Choices

1. Hurricanes originate in the Atlantic Ocean and spin clockwise.

2. A storm surge is determined by the amount of rainfall in a hurricane.

3. Swiftly moving hurricanes are relatively less damaging than immobile ones.

4. Shoreline geography plays a major role in the amount of flooding a hurricane causes.

5. Warm waters are the fuel hurricanes need to feed off for energy and power.

6. The southeastern United States is especially predisposed to hurricanes.

Early Italian Opera

La Scala Opera House in Milan, Italy

Today, like most other kinds of theater and music, the musical drama of opera enjoys myriad forms and interpretations. Operas can exhibit both comical moods as well as the most tragic ones while the actors may be of the highest caliber or simply part-time novices. But it has not always been this way. Since its **inception** in Italy around the year 1600, the opera has experienced a number of shifts and trends. In the beginning, it was heavily influenced by classical Greek drama and attempted to adhere to its heroic subject matter and theme. Yet by the eighteenth century, two distinct forms were beginning to branch out from the original operatic base in Italy. Italian audiences were able to witness two fundamental styles: opera seria and opera buffa. Their distinct styles reflected the social mentality of the era and its ability to morph and grow in a new direction, which later influenced further alterations in modern opera.

The first half of the eighteenth century was dominated by opera seria, which most closely resembled the earliest form of opera. Its characteristics were heavily influenced by the Enlightenment, a period in Europe which put human reason at the forefront of thought. In turn, clarity and structure became the foundation of opera seria. In many ways, simplicity and rational thought, which were further major characteristics of opera seria, go hand in hand. It **eschewed** imagination and improvisation in favor of familiar storylines, most often Greek, which was easier on the audience and did not tax their mental capacities too much. However, some operagoers felt slighted by the fact that operas failed to challenge them, and though it remained a popular form of entertainment, it displayed a number of other limitations.

Some members of the audience found further difficulties with opera seria. First, the organization of the opera never deviated from the usual norm. It was always composed of three acts, and within each act were its fundamental components: recitatives and arias. Recitatives are the singing of the cast, which pushes the action of the opera forward. Arias usually follow as a climax and reveal the emotion or internal conflict of the actors. The main issue was that such a rigid structure made the opera bland and at times predictable. If there had been more flexibility, the operas would have been more vivid and alive, yet the composers were bound by the predominant philosophical constraints of the early 1700s. The stage then was ripe for change in the form of opera buffa, which was beginning to manifest itself within opera seria itself through the intermezzo.

The intermezzo was already an integral part of opera seria in that it was a short performance break between acts and was less predictable than the major production. Over time, the style of the intermezzo caught on and was eventually put on separately, later being dubbed opera buffa. This type of opera was characterized by a light, even comic, motif. More importantly, it was less constrained and displayed elements of free emotion and subject matter that mirrored everyday life, not, for example, heroes from Greek tragedies. Further, music began to play a greater role in the opera, was spontaneous, and often mirrored the emotions of the characters. Because the themes were more true to life, the audience could relate more closely to opera buffa. As it developed, opera buffa also began to take on more serious subject matter yet retained its free-flowing manner.

By the late 1700s, the influence of the Enlightenment was beginning to lose its luster, and the two predominant forms of opera began to merge into one. Opera seria started to display more elasticity in its form and structure and even included some dancing in its performances. Likewise, opera buffa began to engage in more sophisticated themes. By the end of the century, even the most sensitive opera enthusiast could hardly distinguish between the two. More importantly, as each form changed, they were able to provide the audience with the best of both worlds and a more complete opera experience as they were composed with intellectual integrity, stimulation sprinkled with lightheartedness, and humor. From this, the modern form of opera was born.

Glossary
inception: a beginning; a birth
eschew: to avoid

Early Italian Opera

¹→ Today, like most other kinds of theater and music, the musical drama of opera enjoys myriad forms and interpretations. Operas can exhibit both comical moods as well as the most tragic ones while the actors may be of the highest **caliber** or simply part-time novices. But it has not always been this way. Since its **inception** in Italy around the year 1600, the opera has experienced a number of shifts and trends. In the beginning, it was heavily influenced by classical Greek drama and attempted to adhere to its heroic subject matter and theme. Yet by the eighteenth century, two distinct forms were beginning to branch out from the original operatic base in Italy. Italian audiences were able to witness two fundamental styles: opera seria and opera buffa. Their distinct styles reflected the social mentality of the era and its ability to morph and grow in a new direction, which later influenced further alterations in modern opera.

11 The word "caliber" in the passage is closest in meaning to
  Ⓐ size
  Ⓑ experience
  Ⓒ talent
  Ⓓ character

12 According to paragraph 1, two forms in eighteenth-century Italian opera arose because
  Ⓐ it was heavily grounded and influenced by classical domestic drama
  Ⓑ the way people thought was beginning both to develop and change
  Ⓒ traditional themes of heroism were enjoyed by regular audiences
  Ⓓ most opera enthusiasts were demanding a more flexible, exciting style

Glossary
inception: a beginning; a birth

² ➜ The first half of the eighteenth century was dominated by opera seria, which most closely resembled the earliest form of opera. Its characteristics were heavily influenced by **the Enlightenment**, a period in Europe which put human reason at the forefront of thought. In turn, clarity and structure became the foundation of opera seria. In many ways, simplicity and rational thought, which were further major characteristics of opera seria, go hand in hand. It **eschewed** imagination and improvisation in favor of familiar storylines, most often Greek, which was easier on the audience and did not tax their mental capacities too much. However, some operagoers felt slighted by the fact that operas failed to challenge them, and though it remained a popular form of entertainment, it displayed a number of other limitations.

13 The author discusses "the Enlightenment" in paragraph 2 in order to

- Ⓐ note how it was the pinnacle of intellectual thought in Europe
- Ⓑ indicate what was the most responsible for the traits of opera seria
- Ⓒ contrast the structure of opera seria with that of opera buffa
- Ⓓ note that though it was a major social influence, it affected opera little

14 Which of the following can be inferred from paragraph 2 about opera seria?

- Ⓐ It had little connection with the plots or themes of classical Greek drama.
- Ⓑ It was too complicated for the average Italian to comprehend completely.
- Ⓒ It was created by people who were influenced by the Enlightenment.
- Ⓓ It failed to reveal a story ambitious enough to make the audience think.

📖 Glossary
eschew: to avoid

³ → Some members of the audience found further difficulties with opera seria. First, the organization of the opera never deviated from the usual norm. It was always composed of three acts, and within each act were its fundamental components: recitatives and arias. Recitatives are the singing of the cast, which pushes the action of the opera forward. Arias usually follow as a climax and reveal the emotion or internal conflict of the actors. The main issue was that such a rigid structure made the opera bland and at times predictable. If there had been more flexibility, the operas would have been more vivid and alive, yet the composers were bound by the predominant philosophical constraints of the early 1700s. The stage then was ripe for change in the form of opera buffa, which was beginning to manifest itself within opera seria itself through the intermezzo.

15 According to paragraph 3, which of the following is NOT true of the problems with opera seria?

Ⓐ The storyline left few surprises for the audience's benefit.
Ⓑ It regularly followed the same form of recitatives and arias.
Ⓒ The action and imagination of the opera confused the audience.
Ⓓ The composers were, for the most part, bound by social obligation.

⁴ ➔ The intermezzo was already an integral part of opera seria in that it was a short performance break between acts and was less predictable than the major production. Over time, the style of the intermezzo caught on and was eventually put on separately, later being dubbed opera buffa. This type of opera was characterized by a light, even comic, motif. More importantly, it was less constrained and displayed elements of free emotion and subject matter that mirrored everyday life, not, for example, heroes from Greek tragedies. Further, music began to play a greater role in the opera, was spontaneous, and often mirrored the emotions of the characters. Because the themes were more true to life, the audience could relate more closely to opera buffa. As it developed, opera buffa also began to take on more serious subject matter yet retained its free-flowing manner.

16 In paragraph 4, the author discusses "The intermezzo" in order to

Ⓐ note the first time that it was performed
Ⓑ compare its popularity with opera seria
Ⓒ name one of the most famous examples of it
Ⓓ show how it transformed into opera buffa

17 According to paragraph 4, which of the following is true of opera buffa?

Ⓐ Its composers avoided music in favor of a more flexible structure.
Ⓑ Its style and delivery became even more restrained than opera seria.
Ⓒ It was characterized by a serious, heroic motif like Greek drama.
Ⓓ It often featured comedic matters related to everyday life.

By the late 1700s, the influence of the Enlightenment was beginning to lose its luster, and the two predominant forms of opera began to merge into one. Opera seria started to display more elasticity in its form and structure and even included some dancing in its performances. Likewise, opera buffa began to engage in more sophisticated themes. By the end of the century, even the most sensitive opera enthusiast could hardly distinguish between the two. More importantly, as each form changed, they were able to provide the audience with the best of both worlds and a more complete opera experience as they were composed with intellectual integrity, stimulation sprinkled with lightheartedness, and humor. From this, the modern form of opera was born.

18 Which of the sentences below best expresses the essential information in the highlighted sentence in the passage? *Incorrect* answer choices change the meaning in important ways or leave out essential information.

Ⓐ The intellectual integrity, lightheartedness, and humor that the operas were filled with made them the most satisfying form of entertainment.

Ⓑ The changes in both forms of opera allowed the audience to enjoy the musical genre to the utmost by enhancing its quality.

Ⓒ Operas changed in order to become more complete because they no longer satisfied the intellectual and comedic needs of their audiences.

Ⓓ Both forms of opera came to resemble each other with regard to the experience, content, and humor that they provided.

The intermezzo was already an integral part of opera seria in that it was a short performance break between acts and was less predictable than the major production. Over time, the style of the intermezzo caught on and was eventually put on separately, later being dubbed opera buffa. ■ This type of opera was characterized by a light, even comic, motif. ■ More importantly, it was less constrained and displayed elements of free emotion and subject matter that mirrored everyday life, not, for example, heroes from Greek tragedies. ■ Further, music began to play a greater role in the opera, was spontaneous, and often mirrored the emotions of the characters. ■ Because the themes were more true to life, the audience could relate more closely to opera buffa. As it developed, opera buffa also began to take on more serious subject matter yet retained its free-flowing manner.

19 Look at the four squares [■] that indicate where the following sentence could be added to the passage.

For example, a violin might mimic an actor's laughter.

Where would the sentence best fit?

Click on a square [■] to add the sentence to the passage.

20 **Directions:** Complete the table below to summarize the information about operas as discussed in the passage. Match the appropriate statements to the type of opera with which they are associated. TWO answer choices will NOT be used. **This question is worth 3 points.**

Drag your answer choices to the spaces where they belong.
To remove an answer choice, click on it. To review the passage, click on **View Text**.

Answer Choices

1. Its main structure was always composed around three acts.
2. It allowed emotion to be expressed more freely by the actors.
3. It developed out of a short intermission type of production.
4. It was the predominant form of opera in Italy during the early 1700s.
5. It contained climactic arias, which helped move the plot forward.
6. It was constructed around rational thought and simplicity.
7. It was popular in the seventeenth century because of its light subject matter.

Opera seria
-
-
-

Opera buffa
-
-

MEMO

How to Master Skills for the TOEFL® iBT

Actual Test

Answers & Explanations

Second Edition

READING 1

DARAKWON

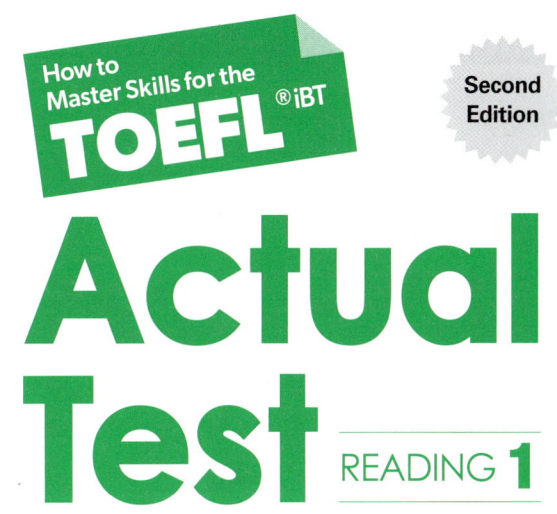

Answers & Explanations

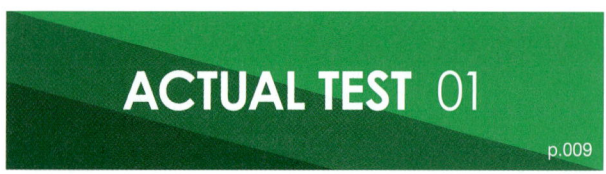

Answers

Passage 1

1. Ⓓ   2. Ⓐ   3. Ⓑ   4. Ⓓ   5. Ⓒ
6. Ⓑ   7. Ⓑ   8. Ⓒ   9. 2
10. 3, 4, 6

Passage 2

11. Ⓓ   12. Ⓑ   13. Ⓑ   14. Ⓐ   15. Ⓐ
16. Ⓒ   17. Ⓐ   18. Ⓒ   19. 1
20. 1, 4, 6

Explanations

Passage 1

1 Negative Factual Information Question

Ⓓ There is no mention in the paragraph of how the printing press created various changes in Europe.

2 Vocabulary Question

Ⓐ When there is a dearth of reading material, there is a lack of it.

3 Factual Information Question

Ⓑ The passage reads, "Handwritten manuscripts were often filled with mistakes as scribes would write down wrong letters or words at times."

4 Rhetorical Purpose Question

Ⓓ The author makes a price comparison in writing, "For instance, a handwritten Bible in the Middle Ages, the period before Gutenberg made his invention, would have cost a person the equivalent of several thousand dollars in modern times. By the time the Protestant Reformation began in the early sixteenth century, the price of a printed Bible only cost around two or three weeks of wages at that time."

5 Reference Question

Ⓒ The "them" that were taken to towns and cities in other locations were the news reports.

6 Factual Information Question

Ⓑ It is written, "Due to the simplicity of the printing press, people around Europe began making their own devices."

7 Sentence Simplification Question

Ⓑ The highlighted sentence notes that the knowledge moved through Europe quickly and became influential due to the printing press. This thought is best expressed in answer choice Ⓑ.

8 Inference Question

Ⓒ In writing, "After the Renaissance came the Reformation, a time when people began breaking with the Catholic Church and formed their own Christian sects, and the Scientific Revolution. These events almost surely would not have happened—or would have happened much more slowly—without the benefit of printing presses to share the ideas people had during those two ages," the author implies that the Scientific Revolution happened when it did because of the printing press.

9 Insert Text Question

2 The sentence before the second square reads, "In places like Venice, which had one of Europe's greatest maritime fleets, ships' captains would frequently carry books, pamphlets, and news reports to other ports, where they would sell the printed material." The sentence to be inserted reads that similar actions happened in Amsterdam, London, and other port cities. The two sentences therefore go well together.

10 Prose Summary Question

3, 4, 6 The passage notes that the printing press influenced Europe for hundreds of years. This thought is best expressed in answer choices 3, 4, and 6. Answer choices 1, 2, and 5 are all minor points, so they are incorrect answers.

Passage 2

11 Vocabulary Question

Ⓓ A characteristic that is innate is inborn in a person or animal.

12 Factual Information Question

Ⓑ The passage reads, "Their astonishing research reveals that these primates exhibit numerous highly developed physical as well as mental characteristics that were previously thought only to be innate in humans."

13 Inference Question

Ⓑ The passage reads, "Chimpanzees are indigenous to Africa, where the tree canopy provides them with shelter, food, and protection," so it can therefore be inferred that the tree canopy is the basis of the chimpanzee's habitat.

14 Rhetorical Purpose Question

Ⓐ The author writes, "Without trees, chimpanzees will become vulnerable to nature's forces and will lack the necessary food sources to keep them viable."

15 Sentence Simplification Question

Ⓐ The highlighted sentence notes that when chimpanzees are isolated, there is less diversity in their genetic pool, which can be harmful. This thought is best expressed in answer choice Ⓐ.

16 Factual Information Question

Ⓒ The passage notes, "As human populations begin to tread on the chimpanzee's habitat, man and primate come into closer contact with each other, exposing the chimpanzee to all kinds of human diseases ranging from the common cold to pneumonia to AIDS."

17 Vocabulary Question

Ⓐ When humans encroach on chimpanzee societies, they invade these societies.

18 Factual Information Question

Ⓒ The writer points out, "The live animal trade only puts money in the pockets of senseless individuals interested in nothing more than their own gains."

19 Insert Text Question

1 The sentence before the first square reads, "To many people, chimpanzees are simply cute, furry, exotic animals—the perfect addition to a home. Infant chimpanzees are taken from their mothers and sold on the black market, which further decreases their numbers in the wild." The sentence to be inserted notes that chimpanzees may be abandoned by their owners when they get older and are no longer novel pets. The two sentences therefore go well together.

20 Prose Summary Question

1, **4**, **6** The passage notes that there are several reasons that the livelihood of chimpanzees is in jeopardy. This thought is best expressed in answer choices **1**, **4**, and **6**. Answer choices **2** and **3** are minor points, so they are wrong. Answer choice **5** contains incorrect information, so it is a wrong answer, too.

p.029

Answers

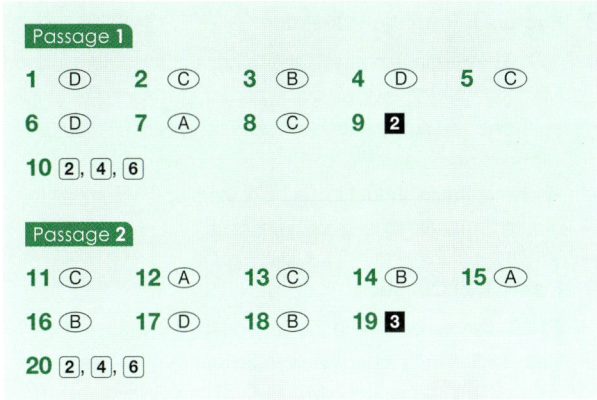

Explanations

1 Vocabulary Question

Ⓓ When Mars is looming as a long-term goal, it is emerging as one.

2 Factual Information Question

Ⓒ The passage notes, "First, they could be future sources of natural resources desperately needed on Earth."

3 Rhetorical Purpose Question

Ⓑ The author of the passage points out that Mars is less life-threatening than the moon in writing, "One major reason a lunar settlement is too hazardous is the contrast between the environments of the moon and the Red Planet. Numerous scientists believe the moon is too difficult for human settlement as compared to Mars."

4 Factual Information Question

Ⓓ The passage points out, "On the other hand, while Mars's atmosphere is significantly thinner than Earth's, at least it has one and would create a slight protective barrier for humans."

5 Sentence Simplification Question

Ⓒ The highlighted sentence points out that due to recent technology, Mars could be a better long-term option than the moon. This point is best expressed in answer choice Ⓒ.

6 Inference Question

Ⓓ In writing, "Conversely, Mars contains vast quantities of water ice, dry ice, and also snow. There is also ample evidence that water once existed on Mars's surface and might return in the future if the planet warms," the author implies that water sources on Mars are not believed to be liquid either above or below the surface.

7 Vocabulary Question

Ⓐ Fertilizing materials are those that are nourishing.

8 Factual Information Question

Ⓒ The passage notes, "Clearly, any future settlements on Mars or the moon will be monumental efforts for the space agencies and astronauts involved. The expenses incurred will be extreme and are a further reason why plans and implementation should focus on the project, which has the greater potential of long-term success."

9 Insert Text Question

❷ The sentence before the second square reads, "If lunar settlements are to be successful, water will be a key component and must be brought with the colonists and continually supplied by further expeditions from Earth, which means they will have a limited capacity of it." The sentence to be inserted points out that any delays in the supplies could put the project and the lives of the colonists in danger. The two sentences therefore go well together.

10 Prose Summary Question

❷, ❹, ❻ The passage notes that settlements on Mars and the moon would be difficult but that those on Mars could sustain life better. This thought is best reflected in answer choices ❷, ❹, and ❻. Answer choice ❶ is a minor point, so it is wrong. In addition, answer choices ❸ and ❺ contain incorrect information, so they are wrong, too.

Passage 2 p.040

11 Rhetorical Purpose Question

Ⓒ The passage notes, "The funeral tradition of the Toraja people on the island of Sulawesi in Indonesia is like no other as it blends the Toraja's ancient animist beliefs with the western influences of Christianity."

12 Factual Information Question

Ⓐ The author writes, "Funeral rites have always played important roles in human history. They typically symbolize a kind of closure of an individual's life on the Earth and provide family and friends the opportunity to pay their respects and to say goodbye."

13 Vocabulary Question

Ⓒ When a family incurs heavy expenses, it sustains those expenses.

14 Factual Information Question

Ⓑ It is written, "The Toraja often begin preparing for their family members' funerals well before they actually die. Sometimes they even start preparations before the member falls ill."

15 Sentence Simplification Question

Ⓐ The highlighted sentence notes that the funeral allows the person who died to enter the next stage of life. This thought is best expressed in answer choice Ⓐ.

16 Inference Question

Ⓑ In writing, "But water buffaloes are not cheap, especially for the Toraja, who are mainly subsistence farmers. Therefore, a family must work months—or sometimes years—to save enough money to purchase a satisfactory number of water buffaloes and other animals, such as pigs, for the funeral ceremony," the author implies that families are under a lot of pressure to raise money for funeral celebrations.

17 Negative Factual Information Question

Ⓓ The passage reads, "Traditional Toraja cemeteries are located in the side of a cliff, where hollowed-out sections are made for families and individuals."

18 Factual Information Question

Ⓑ The author notes, "*Tau tau* are additionally thought to bestow prosperity on the Toraja in general as well as connect them with deceased family members and gods beyond."

19 Insert Text Question

❸ The sentence before the third square reads, "In most Western cultures, this is unheard of since most funeral preparations are made immediately following death." The sentence to be inserted notes that in Western culture, it would be a bad omen to plan a funeral before a person's death. The two sentences therefore go well together.

20 Prose Summary Question

❷, ❹, ❻ The passage notes that the long funeral ceremony of the Toraja releases the dead to the next level of existence. This thought is best reflected in answer choices ❷, ❹, and ❻. Answer choices ❶ and ❸ are minor points, so they are wrong. In addition, answer ❺ contains incorrect information, so it is wrong, too.

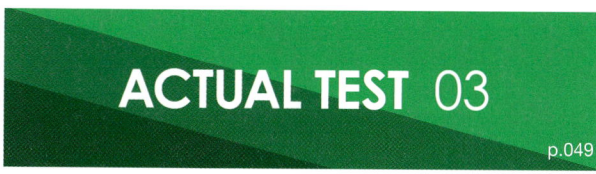

Answers

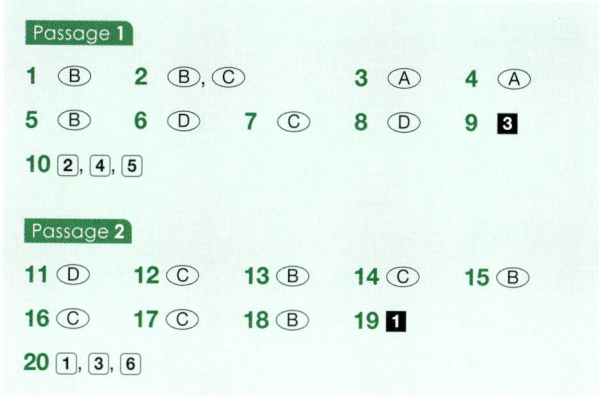

Explanations

Passage 1

1 Inference Question

Ⓑ In writing, "Mangroves are typically found growing along coastlines in tropical and subtropical conditions," the author implies that mangrove trees require hot or warm weather to grow well.

2 Factual Information Question

Ⓑ, Ⓒ The author writes, "All mangroves share the ability to live in salty water and low oxygen conditions," and then adds, "This capability permits some mangroves to grow in water containing two times the salt content of the ocean."

3 Rhetorical Purpose Question

Ⓐ The author makes a comparison in writing, "Some, called non-secreters, create barriers that prevent salt from being absorbed through the process of osmosis, which is how they take in water. Other mangroves, known as secreters, take in salt along with the water they absorb but then undergo a process to remove the salt through pores or salt glands located in their leaves."

4 Sentence Simplification Question

Ⓐ The highlighted sentence notes that mangrove roots changed to let them access oxygen since they get flooded by water and cannot absorb oxygen in the soil. This thought is best expressed in answer choice Ⓐ.

5 Factual Information Question

Ⓑ It is written, "Some of these roots, which can be quite high, keep the trunks of mangroves entirely above water while also providing stability for the trees."

6 Vocabulary Question

Ⓓ When mangrove forests can mitigate the effects of storm surges, they can reduce the effects.

7 Rhetorical Purpose Question

Ⓒ The author writes, "In the water, shrimp, crabs, and lobsters frequently make their homes on the seafloor in mangrove forests."

8 Negative Factual Information Question

Ⓓ There is no mention in the paragraph about which mangrove forests have the most endangered species.

9 Insert Text Question

3 The sentence before the third square reads, "The facts that the trees grow closely together and have complex aboveground root structures help reduce the sizes of waves approaching the shore." The sentence to be inserted adds to this thought by pointing out that one result is that land behind mangrove forests does not get flooded as much as other places. The two sentences therefore go well together.

10 Prose Summary Question

2, 4, 5 The passage notes that mangrove forests are important to their ecosystems for many reasons. This thought is best expressed in answer choices 2, 4, and 5. Answer choice 1 contains information that is not mentioned in the passage, so it is incorrect. Answer choices 3 and 6 are minor points, so they are wrong, too.

Passage 2

11 Vocabulary Question

Ⓓ The crux of a technique is the basis for it.

12 Rhetorical Purpose Question

Ⓒ About headaches, the author writes, "For example, instead of taking aspirin whenever they get headaches, some people go to an acupuncturist to find out what is causing the problem and begin treatments for that specific cause, which will prevent the headaches from returning in the future."

13 Inference Question

Ⓑ The author writes, "In essence, they attempt to treat the source of the health problem rather than simply get rid of the symptoms, which is something that many argue is the flawed crux of Western medicinal techniques," and adds, "Some people go to an acupuncturist to find out what is causing the problem and begin treatments for that specific cause, which will prevent the headaches from returning in the future. In this way, alternative medicine such as acupuncture and herbal therapy have wonderful preventative potential many modern medicines do not."

14 Sentence Simplification Question

Ⓒ The highlighted sentence points out that acupuncturists have the expertise to free up *ki* pathways in the body, which can help patients recover. This thought is best expressed in answer choice Ⓒ.

15 Factual Information Question

Ⓑ The author notes, "Acupuncture is based on ancient Chinese medicine and the importance of *ki*, a kind of life force that pulsates through every human's body."

16 Factual Information Question

Ⓒ It is written, "The ear is considered a highly sensitive area of the human body because it contains a strong, healthy flow of blood as well as numerous nerve points that connect it with the rest of the human body."

17 Negative Factual Information Question

Ⓒ The passage reads, "A second form of alternative therapy based on Chinese traditional medicine is herbal therapy, a process in which special herbs are prescribed by a doctor to be taken in a hot liquid form, usually tea."

18 Inference Question

Ⓑ The author writes, "When it comes to diseases and preventative measures, people should realize that there are many proven alternatives simply to visiting a local Western doctor or hospital to be evaluated and sent home with various prescriptions. In many cases, this type of medicine only masks the essence of the problem while traditional Chinese therapy such as acupuncture and herbal medicine addresses it from the onset." It can therefore be inferred that Western doctors' prescriptions often only address one level of a problem.

19 Insert Text Question

❶ The sentence before the first square reads, "When it comes to diseases and preventative measures, people should realize that there are many proven alternatives simply to visiting a local Western doctor or hospital to be evaluated and sent home with various prescriptions." The sentence to be inserted points out that some illnesses need to be investigated more than that. The two sentences therefore go well together.

20 Prose Summary Question

①, ③, ⑥ The passage notes that people in some countries are turning to traditional medicine instead of using Western medicine. This thought is best reflected in answer choices ①, ③, and ⑥. Answer choices ②, ④, and ⑤ are minor points, so they are wrong.

ACTUAL TEST 04

p.069

Answers

Passage 1

1 Ⓐ   2 Ⓒ   3 Ⓓ   4 Ⓑ   5 Ⓒ
6 Ⓓ   7 Ⓐ   8 Ⓒ   9 ❷
10 ②, ④, ⑤

Passage 2

11 Ⓒ   12 Ⓓ   13 Ⓒ   14 Ⓐ   15 Ⓒ
16 Ⓑ   17 Ⓒ   18 Ⓓ   19 ❸
20 ①, ④, ⑥

Explanations

Passage 1 p.071

1 Vocabulary Question

Ⓐ Delicate temperature requirements are ones that are fragile.

2 Negative Factual Information Question

Ⓒ The passage does not mention that Earth's position between two other planets has an effect on the climate.

3 Reference Question

Ⓓ The "they" that would have influences on temperature and climate are different orbits.

4 Factual Information Question

Ⓑ The passage reads, "As a control element, the computer model maintained Earth's orbital period of 365 days."

5 Sentence Simplification Question

Ⓒ The highlighted passage indicates that astronomers learned that mid-range orbital changes would let Earth sustain life, but people could not live in the same places. This thought is best expressed in answer choice Ⓒ.

6 Vocabulary Question

Ⓓ When the ocean's heat would forestall the return of the ice caps to a great degree, it would prevent that from happening.

6

7 Inference Question

Ⓐ The author writes, "Northern Canada and Russia would become prime real estate," and adds, "At the other extreme, with Earth inside Mercury's orbit and outside Mars's, the temperatures would make life impossible in much of the world, especially the equatorial regions." It can therefore be inferred that most humans would live in the planet's northern regions.

8 Factual Information Question

Ⓒ The passage reads, "At the other extreme, with Earth inside Mercury's orbit and outside Mars's, the temperatures would make life impossible in much of the world, especially the equatorial regions. In a scenario where Earth was closest to the sun in March and April and farthest away in October and November, the temperatures in Africa, India, South America, and Australia would reach almost 200°F, near water's boiling point, in March."

9 Insert Text Question

❷ The sentence before the second square reads, "At the other extreme, with Earth inside Mercury's orbit and outside Mars's, the temperatures would make life impossible in much of the world, especially the equatorial regions." The sentence to be inserted notes that astronomers were unsure about which months Earth would be closest to and farthest from the sun. The two sentences therefore go well together.

10 Prose Summary Question

②, ④, ⑤ The passage notes that changes in Earth's orbit could result in changes to the planet's conditions. This thought is best reflected in answer choices ②, ④, and ⑤. Answer choices ① and ③ contain incorrect information, so they are wrong. In addition, answer choice ⑥ is a minor point, so it is wrong, too.

Passage 2   p.080

11 Rhetorical Purpose Question

Ⓒ The author focuses on a geographical feature by the Nile River in writing, "The Nile River flows northward more than 4,100 miles from central Africa and completes its lengthy journey at the Mediterranean Sea. On the final leg of its trip, it travels through Egypt, where it is surrounded by the Sahara Desert," about the Sahara Desert.

12 Negative Factual Information Question

Ⓓ There is no mention in the paragraph of the starting point of the Nile River.

13 Reference Question

Ⓒ The "they" that deposited soil on the land were the waters of the Nile.

14 Vocabulary Question

Ⓐ When the floodwaters receded, they withdrew from the areas that they covered.

15 Sentence Simplification Question

Ⓒ The highlighted sentence points out that the Egyptians learned to make large and small ships well. This thought is best expressed in answer choice Ⓒ.

16 Factual Information Question

Ⓑ The passage reads, "They employed boats for fishing as well as to transport food from place to place while people additionally sailed up and down the Nile to reach different places."

17 Factual Information Question

Ⓒ The author notes, "The Barque of Amum was maintained at Thebes. It was covered in gold and was decorated with all kinds of ornaments. It—and other ships constructed by the Egyptians—was used for various festivals."

18 Inference Question

Ⓓ In writing, "Deshret, on the other hand, was the hot, dry desert land, which only brought chaos and death to the people," the author implies that few people lived in Deshret in the time of ancient Egypt.

19 Insert Text Question

❸ The sentence before the third square reads, "An alabaster boat was found in the tomb of King Tutankhamun when it was discovered by Howard Carter." The sentence to be inserted focuses on the alabaster boat and describes it as a precious treasure from King Tut's hoard. The two sentences therefore go well together.

20 Prose Summary Question

①, ④, ⑥ The passage notes that the Nile River was of great importance to ancient Egyptian civilization. This thought is best expressed in answer choices ①, ④, and ⑥. Answer choice ② contains information that is not mentioned in the passage, so it is not right. Answer choices ③ and ⑤ are minor points, so they are incorrect, too.

ACTUAL TEST 05

Answers

Passage 1
1 Ⓑ 2 Ⓒ 3 Ⓐ 4 Ⓑ 5 Ⓓ
6 Ⓐ 7 Ⓐ 8 Ⓒ 9 ❷
10 ①, ②, ⑥

Passage 2
11 Ⓓ 12 Ⓑ 13 Ⓑ 14 Ⓒ 15 Ⓑ
16 Ⓐ 17 Ⓑ 18 Ⓐ 19 ❹
20 ②, ④, ⑤

Explanations

Passage 1

1 Negative Factual Information Question
Ⓑ The passage points out, "However, the day when people no longer depend totally on oil may be in sight thanks to the recent development of the hydrogen fuel cell and practical applications for it."

2 Rhetorical Purpose Question
Ⓒ The passage reads, "In fact, the space shuttle used hydrogen fuel cells to produce all of its electricity and water supplies and never had a problem."

3 Factual Information Question
Ⓐ The author notes, "Unfortunately, his subsequent hydrogen fuel cells never produced enough electricity to justify the expense of creating them."

4 Factual Information Question
Ⓑ It is written, "It took Ballard a long time to reach this point since he had difficulty convincing his own managers and investors that he could make the bus."

5 Inference Question
Ⓓ The passage reads, "However, nothing breeds success like success, and once the bus was rolling, Ballard received interest and investment from several major automobile firms. Daimler-Benz produced the first hydrogen cell car in 1997." It can therefore be inferred that he has produced a practical use for the hydrogen fuel cell.

6 Vocabulary Question
Ⓐ When people want to replenish the supply of hydrogen, they want to restock it.

7 Factual Information Question
Ⓐ The passage points out, "Ballard and his team have established another company called Hydrogen General to help develop the infrastructure of hydrogen separation and hydrogen supply points for future fleets of hydrogen-powered cars and buses."

8 Sentence Simplification Question
Ⓒ The highlighted sentence points out that oil companies are not interested in the hydrogen economy because they could lose a lot of money. This thought is best expressed in answer choice Ⓒ.

9 Insert Text Question
❷ The sentence before the second square reads, "California passed a bill in the late 1990s requiring ten percent of cars sold in that state to have zero-emissions of pollutants." The sentence to be inserted points out that the governor ironically used to drive in a Humvee, which used a lot of gas. The two sentences therefore go well together.

10 Prose Summary Question
①, ②, ⑥ The passage points out that there are many obstacles to overcome before the hydrogen economy replaces the petroleum-based one. This thought is best expressed in answer choices ①, ②, and ⑥. Answer choices ③, ④, and ⑤ are all minor points, so they are incorrect.

Passage 2

11 Factual Information Question
Ⓓ It is written, "The decline of the menhaden has had particularly disastrous effects on fish species that feed on it, on bird species that use it as a food source, and on how clean the oceans are."

12 Vocabulary Question
Ⓑ A fish that is not very palatable to humans is not very edible.

13 Vocabulary Question
Ⓑ Epic proportions are those which are massive.

14 Negative Factual Information Question
Ⓒ There is no mention in the paragraph of the desire of people to consume menhaden as food.

15 Sentence Simplification Question

Ⓑ The highlighted sentence points out that the striped bass caught by fishermen in Chesapeake Bay are not as big as those caught in the past. This thought is best expressed in answer choice Ⓑ.

16 Factual Information Question

Ⓐ The author writes, "Entire coastal areas are lifeless as algae kill the fish. Menhaden had reduced the levels of these elements, but now that there are fewer menhaden, algae have taken over."

17 Rhetorical Purpose Question

Ⓑ The passage reads, "Since there is no accurate way to count the number of menhaden in the oceans, they claim that the fewer menhaden are a result of a cyclical event and that the stocks will increase again in time. Yet much of the menhaden catch consists of smaller fish, often less than one year old. These fish have not had a chance to mature long enough to become reproductive, and thus commercial fishing companies are destroying future menhaden stocks to profit at the moment."

18 Factual Information Question

Ⓐ The author comments, "Since there is no accurate way to count the number of menhaden in the oceans, they claim that the fewer menhaden are a result of a cyclical event and that the stocks will increase again in time."

19 Insert Text Question

４ The sentence before the fourth square reads, "Algae grow in great numbers in these conditions, block sunlight, and deplete the water of oxygen." The sentence to be inserted points out another way that algae cause harm in the oceans. The two sentences therefore go well together.

20 Prose Summary Question

２, ４, ５ The passage discusses the harm that the decline of menhaden stocks is causing. This thought is best described in answer choices ２, ４, and ５. Answer choices １ and ３ are minor points, so they are incorrect. Answer choice ６ has incorrect information, so it is also wrong.

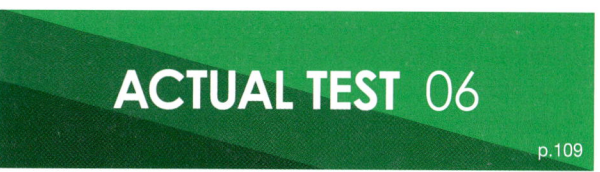

ACTUAL TEST 06

p.109

Answers

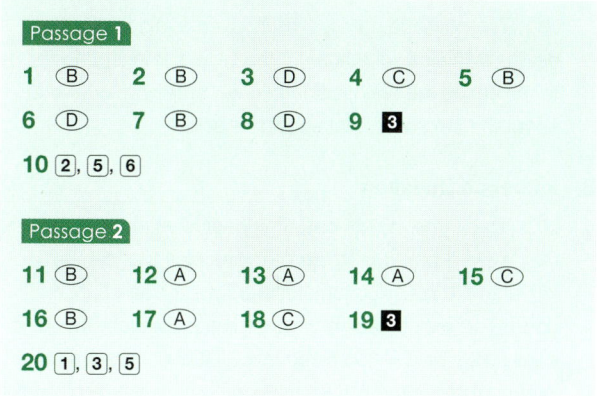

Explanations

Passage 1
p.111

1 Factual Information Question

Ⓑ The passage reads, "Stuttering is the inability to form words or sentences at what is considered a normal speed of speech."

2 Negative Factual Information Question

Ⓑ There is no mention in the passage of a person's gender causing stuttering.

3 Sentence Simplification Question

Ⓓ The highlighted sentence points out that due to practicing for years, the player instinctively performs the action without actually knowing how he did it. This thought is best reflected in answer choice Ⓓ.

4 Factual Information Question

Ⓒ The author writes, "Speech is one of the most complicated actions humans perform with almost every facial muscle, the tongue, the vocal cords, the lungs, and the brain working in concert to create it."

5 Vocabulary Question

Ⓑ Something at the subconscious level of understanding is hidden.

6 Rhetorical Purpose Question

Ⓓ The author focuses on the effectiveness of delayed audio feedback in writing, "For example, a man at a party seems fine talking to people in the crowd, but if he is asked to make a speech, he will freeze up and start to stutter as everyone falls silent to listen to him. His brain now concentrates on what he is saying instead of the other people, and it has more time to think and thus slow down the man's speech patterns. The delayed audio feedback device acts as a substitute for the crowd, bringing noise to the ear as the brain is about to start thinking too much about the next word that should be said."

7 Factual Information Question

Ⓑ The passage notes, "The delayed audio feedback device acts as a substitute for the crowd, bringing noise to the ear as the brain is about to start thinking too much about the next word that should be said."

8 Inference Question

Ⓓ The author points out, "Future studies of the brain may make it possible to create microchips that can be implanted, thereby curing stutterers of their affliction for good. This may smack of science fiction, but for stutterers, it will surely be a welcome advance." It can therefore be inferred that microchips for the brain have not been created or implanted in any stutterers.

9 Insert Text Question

❸ The sentences before the third square reads, "Doctors, speech therapists, and psychologists in the past puzzled over the causes of stuttering and usually determined that it is related to the way a child is brought up or some traumatic incident in childhood." The sentence to be inserted describes a way that children were brought up. The two sentences therefore go well together.

10 Prose Summary Question

②, ⑤, ⑥ The passage points out that past theories on stuttering have been replaced by a new one. This thought is best expressed in answer choices ②, ⑤, and ⑥. Answer choices ① and ③ are minor points, so they are incorrect. Answer choice ④ has incorrect information, so it is also wrong.

Passage 2   p.120

11 Negative Factual Information Question

Ⓑ The paragraph does not mention anything about the types of trees in the forests in Haiti and the Dominican Republic.

12 Rhetorical Purpose Question

Ⓐ The passage reads, "The French decided to import massive numbers of slaves to clear vast forests and to plant sugarcane, a cash crop."

13 Inference Question

Ⓐ The author writes, "The half-million population of Arawak Indians died of disease by 1520, and the Spaniards then imported African slaves." It can therefore be inferred that the Arawak Indians did not live on the island with African slaves.

14 Vocabulary Question

Ⓐ When something has a profound impact, it has a powerful one.

15 Factual Information Question

Ⓒ It is written, "In 1803, the western slaves rebelled and defeated a French expedition to recapture the colony."

16 Factual Information Question

Ⓑ The author writes, "The military was charged with defending the nation's forests and received orders to kill illegal loggers who did not surrender."

17 Sentence Simplification Question

Ⓐ The highlighted sentence points out that Balaguer's policies are still enforced by the Dominican Republic and that they are the most thorough in the Western Hemisphere. This thought is best expressed in answer choice Ⓐ.

18 Factual Information Question

Ⓒ The passage reads, "The already thin soil of Haiti is eroding and blowing away year after year, making farmers' small plots less productive."

19 Insert Text Question

❸ The sentence before the third square reads, "Politically, the Dominicans have had a series of governments concerned about the environmental protection of the nation's forests." The sentence to be inserted describes the actions concerning forests of one of the governments. The two sentences therefore go well together.

20 Prose Summary Question

①, ③, ⑤ The passage notes the Dominican Republic and Haiti have very different forest management policies. This thought is best reflected in answer choices ①, ③, and ⑤. Answer choices ②, ④, and ⑥ are all minor points, so they are wrong.

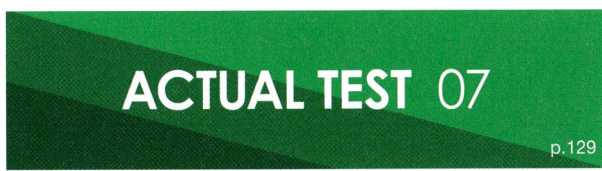

Answers

Passage 1
1 Ⓓ 2 Ⓑ 3 Ⓓ 4 Ⓑ 5 Ⓓ
6 Ⓓ 7 Ⓑ 8 Ⓓ 9 ②
10 ②, ⑤, ⑥

Passage 2
11 Ⓐ 12 Ⓒ 13 Ⓑ 14 Ⓒ 15 Ⓒ
16 Ⓐ 17 Ⓑ 18 Ⓐ 19 ④
20 ②, ③, ⑤

Explanations

Passage 1

1 Inference Question

Ⓓ The author writes, "As a general rule, plants such as trees and flowers begin growing leaves and flowers in spring and develop fully by summer." Due to "as a general rule," it can therefore be inferred that not all plants develop flowers during spring or summer.

2 Factual Information Question

Ⓑ It is written, "The Earth is tilted on its axis, resulting in either the northern or southern half of the planet receiving more direct sunlight from the sun than the other half. As the Earth orbits the sun, which half of the Earth is tilting away from the sun changes and causes the changing of the seasons."

3 Negative Factual Information Question

Ⓓ There is no mention in the paragraph of which season sees the ground receiving the largest amount of sunlight.

4 Reference Question

Ⓑ The "they" that cause plants to behave differently each season are photoreceptors.

5 Sentence Simplification Question

Ⓓ The highlighted sentence notes that photoreceptors activate hormones instructing plants to bloom or lose leaves on account of the amount of light they receive. This thought is best represented in answer choice Ⓓ.

6 Vocabulary Question

Ⓓ When plants stay dormant until spring, they remain inactive.

7 Rhetorical Purpose Question

Ⓑ The author uses peach trees as an example of plants that blossom depending on how cold the weather is in writing, "Some plants, such as peach trees, are capable of measuring the temperature. They can tell how warm or cold the air is and for how long it remains at a certain temperature. When there are only a certain number of cold hours in a day, an internal signal may be sent to peach trees that enables them to blossom."

8 Factual Information Question

Ⓓ The author comments, "Yet another way that some plants determine the changing of the seasons is by monitoring the amount of darkness each day," and then writes, "Short-day plants, which include chrysanthemums, poinsettias, violets, rice, and soybeans, flower when days are shorter."

9 Insert Text Question

② The sentence before the second square reads, "Summer features long days full of sunlight and warm temperatures, which are ideal conditions for photosynthesis." The sentence to be inserted describes the process of photosynthesis. The two sentences therefore go well together.

10 Prose Summary Question

②, ⑤, ⑥ The passage notes that plants can detect seasonal changes in various ways. This thought is best expressed in answer choices ②, ⑤, and ⑥. Answer choice ① contains incorrect information, so it is wrong. Answer choices ③ and ④ are minor points, so they are incorrect, too.

Passage 2

11 Vocabulary Question

Ⓐ When knowledge is transmitted to others, it is passed on.

12 Negative Factual Information Question

Ⓒ There is no mention in the paragraph of the use of telescopes for navigation.

13 Inference Question

Ⓑ The author writes, "These satellites are in fixed positions, so by reading a signal from three of them, a person holding a GPS receiver can know his precise location." It can therefore be inferred that a GPS receiver will always be in range of at least three satellites.

14 Sentence Simplification Question

Ⓒ The highlighted sentence notes that the first Russian satellite launch made scientists realize that satellites could assist with navigation. That thought is best expressed in answer choice Ⓒ.

15 Factual Information Question

Ⓒ The passage reads, "By 1964, four American satellites were being used to help American naval vessels navigate. Called Transit, the system took up to ninety minutes to give a position report, which was too slow for ever-changing battlefield situations."

16 Factual Information Question

Ⓐ The passage reads, "Unfortunately, the Navy, the Air Force, and the Army competed to build different systems, wasting resources and time by creating three systems instead of one."

17 Factual Information Question

Ⓑ It is written, "The military, afraid that rival countries and civilians would use the system to attack the United States or for criminal purposes, installed a distortion in the GPS signal that led to a slight error in civilian GPS receivers."

18 Rhetorical Purpose Question

Ⓐ The author writes, "By the turn of the century, GPS receiving devices became more inexpensive and are now affordable for much of the public."

19 Insert Text Question

❹ The sentence before the fourth square reads, "By 1978, the system was ready and being tested, and the eventual cost of the system was four billion dollars." The sentence to be inserted describes what the creator of GPS did after the system was built. The two sentences therefore go well together.

20 Prose Summary Question

②, ③, ⑤ The passage notes that the American military was important in creating and operating GPS. This thought is best expressed in answer choices ②, ③, and ⑤. Answer choices ①, ④, and ⑥ are all minor points, so they are incorrect.

ACTUAL TEST 08

Answers

Passage 1
1 Ⓓ   2 Ⓐ   3 Ⓒ   4 Ⓑ   5 Ⓓ
6 Ⓒ   7 Ⓑ   8 Ⓐ   9 ❹
10 ①, ④, ⑥

Passage 2
11 Ⓓ   12 Ⓓ   13 Ⓑ   14 Ⓑ   15 Ⓓ
16 Ⓓ   17 Ⓑ   18 Ⓒ   19 ❶
20 ①, ⑤, ⑥

Explanations

Passage 1

1 Sentence Simplification Question

Ⓓ The highlighted sentence notes that all fish help one another survive in that they stop bacteria from expanding too much. This thought is best expressed in answer choice Ⓓ.

2 Inference Question

Ⓐ The passage reads, "Though many types of fish are continually stalking and evading one another for survival, they all band together in an attempt to keep bacteria levels at bay in order to enable their own existence to continue." It can therefore be inferred that if bacteria increase in number, they can be harmful to fish.

3 Rhetorical Purpose Question

Ⓒ The author writes, "On the one hand, they are beneficial as they stimulate plant life through food decomposition, which releases chemicals necessary for the growth of plant life. This is called nutrient recycling and helps keep the oceans alive."

4 Factual Information Question

Ⓑ It is written, "In water, bacteria prove to be an even greater threat than on land because as they proliferate, they reduce the oxygen levels necessary for organisms in the oceans to live."

5 Vocabulary Question

Ⓓ When bacteria levels become debilitating, they are devastating to an ecosystem.

6 Negative Factual Information Question

Ⓒ There is no mention in the passage that phagocytes help weakened cells revive.

7 Factual Information Question

Ⓑ The passage notes, "By ridding the ocean of weaker fish, predators allow the stronger ones to multiply, making their species stronger and more resilient."

8 Reference Question

Ⓐ The "it" that does not merely provide a food source for a dominant species is this way of life.

9 Insert Text Question

■4 The sentence before the fourth square reads, "It also maintains a healthy level of bacteria in an ocean's ecosystem, thus ensuring the continuation of all species of life within that ecosystem." The sentence to be inserted notes that fish are helping themselves by consuming one another. The two sentences therefore go well together.

10 Prose Summary Question

1, 4, 6 The passage notes that bacteria are a danger to ocean ecosystems and that if there were no predators, bacteria would be a serious hazard to ocean life. This thought is best represented in answer choices 1, 4, and 6. Answer choices 2, 3, and 5 are all minor points and are therefore incorrect.

Passage 2   p.159

11 Sentence Simplification Question

Ⓓ The highlighted sentence notes that some people's claims to have common ancestors cannot be verified because the ancestors are mythical or prehistoric. This thought is best expressed in answer choice Ⓓ.

12 Rhetorical Purpose Question

Ⓓ It is written, "Sometimes groups of people will claim a common ancestor but be unable to prove the connection either because the claims are rooted more in myth than in fact or because the common ancestor is believed to have existed before the advent of written records within those groups' cultures. Such groups are not considered lineages but clans."

13 Factual Information Question

Ⓑ The author notes, "This is especially easy today thanks to online genealogy sites, many of which allow users to search through a database of pre-researched lineages to see if their own has already been traced by someone else."

14 Factual Information Question

Ⓑ The author writes, "Today, individuals, driven by an urge to learn more about their family's history or by a desire to find a connection to someone historically important, often trace their personal lineages through online genealogy sites."

15 Rhetorical Purpose Question

Ⓓ It is written, "Similarly, patrilineal descent is often used in monarchies to determine who has the best claim on the throne."

16 Vocabulary Question

Ⓓ Rules prohibiting incest forbid it.

17 Vocabulary Question

Ⓑ When regular DNA is diluted, it is reduced in amount.

18 Factual Information Question

Ⓒ It is written, "Unlike regular DNA, mitochondrial DNA is passed down exclusively from mother to child."

19 Insert Text Question

■1 The sentence before the first square reads, "Lineages can also be used to unearth the common roots of various ethnic groups." The sentence to be inserted notes a problem with attempting to unearth common roots. The two sentences therefore go well together.

20 Prose Summary Question

1, 5, 6 The passage notes that lineage was important historically and that even today, people are interested in knowing their own lineage. This thought is best expressed in answer choices 1, 5, and 6. Answer choice 2 has incorrect information, and answer choice 3 is a minor point, so they are incorrect. Answer choice 4 has information not in the passage, so it is also wrong.

ACTUAL TEST 09

p.167

Answers

Passage 1

1 Ⓐ	2 Ⓑ	3 Ⓓ	4 Ⓐ	5 Ⓒ
6 Ⓑ	7 Ⓒ	8 Ⓑ	9 ▣2	
10 ①, ②, ⑤				

Passage 2

11 Ⓓ	12 Ⓓ	13 Ⓐ	14 Ⓑ	15 Ⓒ
16 Ⓒ	17 Ⓒ	18 Ⓓ	19 ▣3	
20 ②, ⑤, ⑥				

Explanations

Passage 1 p.169

1 Factual Information Question

Ⓐ It is written, "By far the largest percentage of the atmosphere is comprised of the gas nitrogen, which makes up approximately seventy-eight percent of the planet's atmosphere."

2 Inference Question

Ⓑ In writing, "Nitrogen is vital both to plants and animals. For instance, plants require nitrogen to create chlorophyll, which is utilized in the process of photosynthesis, from which plants obtain both food and energy," the author implies that nitrogen is needed for plants to make their own food.

3 Rhetorical Purpose Question

Ⓓ The author points out the role of diazotrophs in nitrogen fixation in writing, "This happens during the first stage of the nitrogen cycle, which is called fixation. Diazotrophs are nitrogen-fixing bacteria in the soil that contain an enzyme known as nitrogenase. It is this enzyme that permits nitrogen to combine with hydrogen to form ammonia, but this can only happen when there is no oxygen present."

4 Rhetorical Purpose Question

Ⓐ The author shows two ways that nature can create nitrite in writing, "Interestingly, lightning strikes and volcanic eruptions are so powerful that they are capable of transforming N_2 into NO_2."

5 Negative Factual Information Question

Ⓒ There is no mention in the paragraph of where the most lightning strikes hit the ground.

6 Sentence Simplification Question

Ⓑ The highlighted sentence points out that animals benefit when they eat the plants, which contain different acids. This thought is best expressed in answer choice Ⓑ.

7 Vocabulary Question

Ⓒ The fact that the atmosphere has a finite amount of nitrogen means that it is limited.

8 Factual Information Question

Ⓑ The author writes, "The fifth stage, called denitrification, happens due to the actions of anaerobic bacteria, which are bacteria that are active only when there is no oxygen."

9 Insert Text Question

▣2 The sentence before the second square reads, "Other times, the ammonia may be changed so that it reenters the atmosphere." The sentence to be inserted points out that this action—and another one—may take place depending upon the type of bacteria acting on the nitrates and the ammonia. The two sentences therefore go well together.

10 Prose Summary Question

①, ②, ⑤ The passage notes that the nitrogen cycle shows the changes in forms of nitrogen as it moves from the air to the ground. This thought is best expressed in answer choices ①, ②, and ⑤. Answer choices ③, ④, and ⑥ are all minor points, so they are incorrect answer choices.

Passage 2 p.178

11 Factual Information Question

Ⓓ The passage reads, "Previously, wild flocks spent the warmer parts of the year in their native habitat of northern Canada, and, around August, they made the 2,500-mile southerly journey to the gulf coast of Texas in the United States."

12 Negative Factual Information Question

Ⓓ People did not hunt whooping cranes for sport due to their great size.

13 Sentence Simplification Question

Ⓐ The highlighted sentence notes that whooping cranes raised by humans have no parental guidance, which is a problem when they need to migrate south. This thought is best expressed in answer choice Ⓐ.

14

14 Factual Information Question

ⓑ It is written, "Additionally, during frigid seasons, food sources become scarce, and migration to more fertile feeding grounds becomes mandatory for their survival."

15 Rhetorical Purpose Question

ⓒ The author writes, "Still, like all migratory birds, they have a natural instinct called imprinting. This means they will follow and trust the first object they open their eyes to. This theory laid the groundwork for the conservationists' imaginative plan of aircraft-led migration. Humans act like parents with ultralight aircraft and allow young whooping cranes to imprint on them as if they were their natural parents."

16 Reference Question

ⓒ The "they" that will follow and trust the first object they open their eyes to are whooping cranes.

17 Factual Information Question

ⓒ The author writes, "The main issue is that migration is learned from the young chick's parents, and in most cases, whooping cranes born in captivity have none. Still, like all migratory birds, they have a natural instinct called imprinting. This means they will follow and trust the first object they open their eyes to. This theory laid the groundwork for the conservationists' imaginative plan of aircraft-led migration."

18 Vocabulary Question

ⓓ When there are few hitches, there are few difficulties.

19 Insert Text Question

③ The sentence before the third square reads, "Fortunately, the whooping crane, like other endangered species such as the bald eagle, ultimately became a protected species by federal law." The sentence to be inserted provides an example of how the law is applied to people who break it. The two sentences therefore go well together.

20 Prose Summary Question

②, ⑤, ⑥ The passage notes that the whooping crane is endangered but is making a comeback thanks to conservationists. This thought is best expressed in answer choices ②, ⑤, and ⑥. Answer choices ①, ③, and ④ are minor points, so they are all incorrect.

ACTUAL TEST 10

p.187

Answers

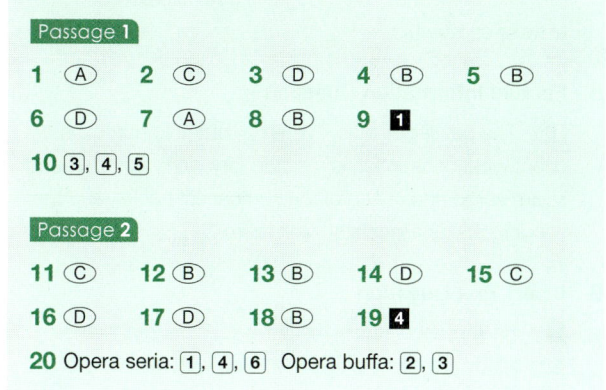

Passage 1				
1 Ⓐ	2 Ⓒ	3 Ⓓ	4 Ⓑ	5 Ⓑ
6 Ⓓ	7 Ⓐ	8 Ⓑ	9 ①	
10 ③, ④, ⑤				

Passage 2				
11 Ⓒ	12 Ⓑ	13 Ⓑ	14 Ⓓ	15 Ⓒ
16 Ⓓ	17 Ⓓ	18 Ⓑ	19 ④	
20 Opera seria: ①, ④, ⑥ Opera buffa: ②, ③				

Explanations

Passage 1   p.189

1 Vocabulary Question

Ⓐ When winds eclipse certain speeds, they exceed those speeds.

2 Factual Information Question

Ⓒ It is written, "Due to minimal high atmospheric winds, those near the surface of the water begin to spin and spiral in a counterclockwise direction, feeding on the heat from the ocean."

3 Inference Question

Ⓓ The passage reads, "They manifest themselves in the warm waters of the Atlantic Ocean and the eastern Pacific Ocean, usually in the form of a low-pressure weather system." It can therefore be inferred that they are not likely to occur in cool oceanic areas.

4 Factual Information Question

Ⓑ The author writes, "The size of the surge itself is determined by the slope of the shore, called the continental shelf, out into the ocean. If the slope is steep, the storm surge will not be as great as when it is shallower, which causes a more powerful surge due to the fact that the ocean's depth is not great enough to absorb the energy and the massive amounts of water."

5 Rhetorical Purpose Question

Ⓑ The author comments, "Another major contributor to the measure of destruction that is caused is the movement of a hurricane. The speed of a hurricane as it makes landfall and moves inland is a major deciding factor for the extent of the damage it causes."

6 Negative Factual Information Question
Ⓓ It is not true that all coastlines are affected by the storm surge of a hurricane.

7 Sentence Simplification Question
Ⓐ The highlighted passage points out that flooding causes problems in a large area and is the most destructive part of a hurricane. This thought is best expressed in answer choice Ⓐ.

8 Factual Information Question
Ⓑ The passage notes, "When it comes to hurricanes, direct wind destruction is a secondary worry compared to storm surge, the speed of the hurricanes' tracks, and the flooding that is associated with them."

9 Insert Text Question
1 The sentence before the first square reads, "While high winds are commonly associated with the perils of hurricanes, the most destructive factor is the accompanying storm surge as it strikes land." The sentence to be inserted points out another factor that can make a storm surge more powerful. The two sentences therefore go well together.

10 Prose Summary Question
3, **4**, **5** The passage notes that the directional speed and storm surge of a hurricane are its two most destructive aspects. This thought is best expressed in answer choices **3**, **4**, and **5**. Answer choice **1** contains incorrect information, so it is wrong. Answer choices **2** and **6** are minor points, so they are also wrong.

Passage 2   p.197

11 Vocabulary Question
Ⓒ An actor of the highest caliber has talent.

12 Factual Information Question
Ⓑ The passage reads, "Their distinct styles reflected the social mentality of the era and its ability to morph and grow in a new direction, which later influenced further alterations in modern opera."

13 Rhetorical Purpose Question
Ⓑ The author writes, "The first half of the eighteenth century was dominated by opera seria, which most closely resembled the earliest form of opera. Its characteristics were heavily influenced by the Enlightenment."

14 Inference Question
Ⓓ The passage reads, "In many ways, simplicity and rational thought, which were further major characteristics of opera seria, go hand in hand. It eschewed imagination and improvisation in favor of familiar storylines, most often Greek, which was easier on the audience and did not tax their mental capacities too much." It can therefore be inferred that opera seria did not have stories ambitious enough to make the audience think.

15 Negative Factual Information Question
Ⓒ It is not true that the action and imagination of the opera confused the audience.

16 Rhetorical Purpose Question
Ⓓ The passage reads, "The intermezzo was already an integral part of opera seria in that it was a short performance break between acts and was less predictable than the major production. Over time, the style of the intermezzo caught on and was eventually put on separately, eventually being dubbed opera buffa."

17 Factual Information Question
Ⓓ The passage reads, "This type of opera was characterized by a light, even comic, motif. More importantly, it was less constrained and displayed elements of free emotion and subject matter that mirrored everyday life, not, for example, heroes from Greek tragedies."

18 Sentence Simplification Question
Ⓑ The highlighted sentence notes that both forms of opera improved its quality and let the audience enjoy the genre very much. This thought is best expressed in answer choice Ⓑ.

19 Insert Text Question
4 The sentence before the fourth square reads, "Further, music began to play a greater role in the opera, was spontaneous, and often mirrored the emotions of the characters." The sentence to be inserted provides an example of music playing a greater role in opera. The two sentences therefore go well together.

20 Fill in a Table Question
Opera seria: **1**, **4**, **6**   Opera buffa: **2**, **3**
About opera seria, the author notes, "It was always composed of three acts," and adds, "The first half of the eighteenth century was dominated by opera seria." The author further writes, "In turn, clarity and structure became the foundation of opera seria. In many ways, simplicity and rational thought, which were further major characteristics of opera seria, go hand in hand." As for opera buffa, the author writes, "The intermezzo was already an integral part of opera seria in that it was a short performance break between acts and was less predictable than the major production. Over time, the style of the intermezzo caught on and was eventually put on separately, later being dubbed opera buffa.", and, "More importantly, it was less constrained and displayed elements of free emotion and subject matter that mirrored everyday life, not, for example, heroes from Greek tragedies."

Actual Test
READING 1